# TILL DEATH DO US PART

---

DANIEL H. GILBERTSON
& DOUGLAS E. O'NEILL

Copyright © 2023 Daniel H. Gilbertson & Douglas E. O'Neill

All rights reserved. No part of this book may be reproduced, stored, or transmitted by any means—whether auditory, graphic, mechanical, or electronic—without written permission of both publisher and author, except in the case of brief excerpts used in critical articles and reviews. Unauthorized reproduction of any part of this work is illegal and is punishable by law.

ISBN: 979-8-88640-445-6 (sc)
ISBN: 979-8-88640-446-3 (hc)
ISBN: 979-8-88640-447-0 (e)

Because of the dynamic nature of the Internet, any web addresses or links contained in this book may have changed since publication and may no longer be valid. The views expressed in this work are solely those of the author and do not necessarily reflect the views of the publisher, and the publisher hereby disclaims any responsibility for them.

One Galleria Blvd., Suite 1900, Metairie, LA 70001
1-888-421-2397

This book is dedicated to all those who have
lost a loved one and found love again.

In loving memory of Patricia Ann Gilbertson
and Demetra Lynette O'Neill

And, of course, our gratitude to Patty Linn
Gilbertson and Mary O'Neill, our loving wives who
understand the importance of this endeavor.

"It is the story that matters not just the ending."

—Paul Lockhart

# Contents

Introduction .................................................................... vii
Preface .............................................................................. ix

## PART 1
## My Wife Is Dying

Chapter 1   Diagnosis ........................................................ 3
Chapter 2   Telling the Children ...................................... 7
Chapter 3   Telling Others .............................................. 13
Chapter 4   Questioning – What Do We Do Now? ...... 15
Chapter 5   Seeking Information ................................... 17
Chapter 6   Making Tough Decisions ........................... 19
Chapter 7   Staying in the Hospital ............................... 23
Chapter 8   Undergoing Treatment ............................... 27
Chapter 9   Coming Home ............................................ 32
Chapter 10  Talking about the Future .......................... 34

## PART 2
## Dealing with Our Wives' Deaths

Chapter 11  The Final Days ........................................... 43
Chapter 12  The Days After Death ................................ 51
Chapter 13  The Funeral ................................................ 57
Chapter 14  Returning to Life "Alone" ......................... 62
Chapter 15  Grief ............................................................ 65

# PART 3
# Starting Over

Chapter 16  Child Care .................................................................71

Chapter 17  Back to Work ............................................................73

Chapter 18  Schedules...................................................................75

Chapter 19  Bills...........................................................................77

Chapter 20  Paperwork .................................................................79

Chapter 21  Personal Belongings...................................................82

Chapter 22  What Is a Widower? ..................................................84

Chapter 23  Emotions and Stress..................................................89

Chapter 24  Single Parenthood .....................................................94

# PART 4
# Dating Again

Chapter 25  Dating - Anxiety..................................................... 105

Chapter 26  Dating - Readiness ..................................................107

Chapter 27  Dating - Changes in the Dating Scene....................109

Chapter 28  Dating - We've Changed! ........................................112

Chapter 29  Dating - Motivation: What Are You Looking For? ... 115

Chapter 30  Dating - Children's Concerns ................................. 119

Chapter 31  Dating - Other People's Opinions...........................123

Chapter 32  Dating - Sex and Intimacy......................................125

Chapter 33  Dating: The Kids and the New Person in the Family....127

Chapter 34  Dating - So Now What?..........................................129

Chapter 35  No Longer a Widower.............................................130

Acknowledgments .......................................................................133

# Introduction

Doug and Dan met in a classroom at South Dakota State University. Doug was teaching a geography class, and Dan was one of his students. Through their conversations, they found common ground in that they had just lost their wives, and at home were young children who needed care and guidance. They were widowers. But surely they were not alone. While they faced unique experiences and perilous times, they realized there must be other men out there in their situation. Right then, Doug and Dan decided to share their journey as they muddled their way through what seemed like "the worst of times."

# Preface

The following is structured around a concept Dan and Doug had from the onset. The book would be built on the premise of friends talking over several cups of coffee at a quiet café.

# Part 1
# MY WIFE IS DYING

Ecclesiastes 3:2
"A time to be born and a time to die"

## Chapter 1

# DIAGNOSIS

### DOUG AND DEMETRA

Our nightmare started one bright fall day in 1988. Our sixth child, Laurel, was but four months old. While nursing Laurel, Demetra noticed a lump in her left breast. She first thought it was just a blocked milk duct, but when nursing became increasingly difficult, Demetra went to her doctor for a consultation. He immediately recognized the lump as more than a clogged milk duct and recommended a biopsy.

The biopsy was done and the lump removed on the Friday before Thanksgiving. As soon as Demetra and I walked into the doctor's office and looked at his face, we both knew the lump was cancerous. The doctor said the cancer had probably spread to her lymph nodes. He recommended a mastectomy. Because we had already discussed what we might do in this situation, we agreed that was our best option. We scheduled it for the Monday after Thanksgiving. We found it very difficult to feel thankful that year.

## DAN AND PATTY

One day in early fall of 1985, I came home from work to find Patty sitting in a chair with a big smile on her face and a card for me in her hand. We did not often give each other cards, so I was pretty surprised to get one. I couldn't think of anything special I had done recently, so when I opened and read the card, I was shocked. There was a handwritten note on the bottom of the card that read, "We're going to have a baby!" I can still see that radiant smile on Patty's face.

I was ecstatic. We embraced and cried tears of joy. It was a dream-come-true for both of us. Patty had suffered a miscarriage in June of that year, and we were unsure if she could ever get pregnant again. Patty had two children from a previous marriage, but this child would be ours, together. We immediately called our families and friends with the good news. No one could have foreseen what would happen next.

A few days later, Patty's doctor called. He said some of her blood counts were unusually high, and he recommended she come in for more tests. While at the doctor's office, he asked her if she had been feeling overly tired, but Patty said no. She had been feeling fine. Patty told him that we had just moved into our new home and getting settled was a big job, but she didn't feel any more tired than usual. The doctor told her to go home, rest, and come in the next day for another blood test.

 **From Patty's journal that day, October 10:** *I wasn't too concerned about the test, and I went to the clinic with no worries.*

After Patty's second round of blood tests, her doctor said that her white blood count was four times higher than it should be. Thinking about leukemia, he was concerned enough to refer her to an oncology specialist in Sioux Falls (about 50 miles away), so she could have a bone marrow test. He added that it was possible the count was high because of the pregnancy.

**Her journal continues:** *I went home crying because I had always associated bone marrow tests with cancer. My appointment was early the next week and by the time we went down for the test, everyone had me convinced that it couldn't be cancer. Dan, the children, Mom, Donna (my mother-in-law), several friends, and I had done some checking into leukemia, and I just didn't have the symptoms for it.*

Patty and I were very concerned about what this could be. Every worst-case possibility ran through our heads. It was obvious that Patty was very stressed. I constantly tried to reassure her that everything would be fine. But even though I tried not to show it, I was just as uncertain and frightened as she was.

**Patty, a few days later:** *I wasn't afraid of the test at all because my primary doctor said it would only be a little uncomfortable. The test didn't last long—but it hurt! Thank God it didn't last long.*

The oncology specialist told us the test was to confirm or rule out the possibility of leukemia. He also said that because Patty's white blood count was so high, he didn't think the pregnancy could be the cause. He said the results would be ready the next day. When Patty called the clinic the following day, they said to come in after we got home from work. The doctor would discuss the results at that point. Before we left, I told Patty that I felt really good about everything, and I was sure she was fine. We had a hot fudge sundae before we went to the clinic.

*On the way to the clinic, I was thinking that our lives might never be the same. I couldn't have been more right! But I had convinced myself that something was wrong with the baby, and we wouldn't be able to have children.*

The doctor told us that Patty had "an unusual type of leukemia, chronic granulocytic leukemia, also known as chronic myelocytic leukemia (CML)."

 *My first thought was, our baby!*

My first thought was, "My wife is going to die."

I broke down, and Patty seemed to be in shock. Patty squeezed my hand for dear life. The doctor gave us a minute to collect ourselves, and then he talked to us about the treatment. We left the clinic feeling devastated.

 *How ironic—as we left the doctor's office, we ran into my best friend, Dee, in the hall of the clinic. She tried to stop us to chat, but Dan mumbled something about calling her that evening. Neither of us could talk.*

## Chapter 2

# TELLING THE CHILDREN

**DOUG AND DEMETRA**

When Demetra was diagnosed, our six children ranged in age from five months to twelve years of age: Heather-12, Erik-9, Jaimie-7, Sean-6, Brittany-3, and Laurel-5 months. It was difficult for me to tell them their mother had cancer and would need surgery because I wasn't sure how I felt myself. I guess the best way to describe it would be confused, fearful, and angry, since I was being forced to consider a future that looked uncertain and chaotic. Although the oldest two children understood the seriousness of their mother's situation, I felt unable to adequately explain to them the changes that would likely take place in their lives and that of Demetra's. The younger children could not grasp the long-term consequences of their mother's illness. For them, it was a case of explaining how some "owie-boo-boos" can make Mommy real sick, and she would have to go to the hospital to get help.

When Demetra and I sat them down and spoke about her illness for the first time, we realized how unsure we were about where this was all going. We couldn't know the future and couldn't give the children any reassurances.

**From Demetra's journal:** *It seems I may not have lots of time left. There are so many things to say and do; I don't know where to start.*

*Sean, one day you asked when I was going to get a real job, believe me, this has been a real job.*

*Heather, you have so much potential. Not only are you intelligent, but you're pretty as well. Don't let bitterness take over your life.*

*Erik, just because something isn't easy doesn't mean it isn't worthwhile.*

*Jaimie, what are we going to do with you? You are so lazy, I hope I live long enough to see you change that.*

*Heather cried several times, but I think she feels better because of it. I said, "Heather, at least I have a sense of humor." Heather said, "It's kind of different, your humor. At least you're not an old stiff as a mom." I replied, "No I'm not, but I will be someday."*

## DAN AND PATTY

At first, we didn't think we should tell the children. Our initial parental instinct was to protect them from the emotional turmoil. They were so young—Alisha was nine and Brett just six. Patty and I wanted to keep their lives as normal as possible. After much discussion, we decided it was best, after all, to tell them straight off. They knew we were sad, but neither child really understood. They could not have fathomed what lay ahead of them.

We decided to take Alisha and Brett to the library to help us gather more information about leukemia. After the library, we went to Patty's parents' house.

**From Patty's journal, October 15:** *I hugged Mom and Dad and couldn't help but cry. It was the first time I had ever seen Dad cry. It meant so much to see how much they cared, but I also felt so bad to see them hurting.*

Not long after we returned home, Patty's brother David called. He lived in Alabama, but told Patty that he'd come in a second if she needed him.

*I've never known him to call me. Tragedy seems to bring families closer. Everyone's reaction was the same—disbelief.*

The following week, we went back to Sioux Falls to consult with the oncology specialist.

**October 23:** *The week went by much too fast. We had done a lot of reading and were hoping I had a type of leukemia where I could go into remission and live for many years. I was very afraid for our baby. I was so sure that I would have to have immediate chemotherapy and thus would have to abort the baby. Rea and Dee went to Sioux Falls with Dan and me. Right before we went in, I wanted so badly to turn around and run! I didn't want to know anything more!*

*The doctor said I didn't have to have chemotherapy until as late in the pregnancy as possible. He said I would never have a complete remission, but as my white blood count got worse that I would need the chemo to keep a "lid" on the disease. He said the chemo would be a slight risk towards the baby (causing a birth defect or it may abort the baby). But he also said there was a slim possibility I could go through the entire pregnancy without needing chemo. Dan and I both agreed if there was a chance of having a normal baby that we couldn't abort it.*

# MY WIFE IS DYING

*The doctor told us the average person lives three to five years with this type of leukemia. At first, it didn't even bother me because I was so thankful that we could have our baby. He explained the drugs they would be using. Then I was so afraid of being hospitalized, being violently sick, and losing my hair.*

*When we told everyone the news, I think they were shocked, but since I appeared to be taking it so well, they did, too. All we told the children was that we were going to try to have the baby and that I wouldn't be sick for a while.*

*But every night, lying in bed, everything seemed so much worse. I would cry until I went to sleep. When we first found out, Dan would cry with me and hold me in his arms. At times it was so hard to be close to him because I couldn't stand the thought of being without him. After about a week, Dan quit crying. He would still comfort me, but he wasn't showing his emotions. I am not sure if he isn't facing up to the cancer or maybe he's more hopeful than I am.*

*Just when I think I am managing, I think about leaving Dan and the children, and I start crying all over again. I just can't imagine dying right now . . . and being at peace.*

Things got even more complicated as one day after Patty and I got home from work, the baby-sitter told us that Alisha had been crying and was very upset. Up to that point, it appeared to us that Alisha was handling her mother's cancer well. But that was not the case. Alisha admitted that she was scared of her mother dying and said she was afraid that she would be separated from the baby if her mother died. Apparently, Alisha's birth father had told her that she and Brett would go live with him when their mother died.

Alisha had also confessed to the sitter that she was too embarrassed to talk to us about her mother's illness. She had sensed that we weren't telling her all we knew about Patty's cancer. Of course, this made us feel absolutely terrible. I suggested that we take Alisha to Sioux Falls for Patty's next doctor appointment.

When we took Alisha out of school to go to Sioux Falls, she was thrilled not only because she was able to skip school but also because she was being involved. We talked all the way, and Alisha seemed to feel better. She also was invited into the conference room and got to listen to everything the doctor had to say. For a nine-year-old, that day she was very mature.

*November 20: I told Alisha it was okay to feel scared and to cry because I felt the same way at times. I also told her I didn't know when I was going to die, but that I felt fine right now, and I would try to be more open with her from now on.*

After that, our relationship with Alisha was so much better. There were no secrets between us. Everything was out in the open. If Alisha was concerned about something, she knew she could talk to us about it. She became a part of what was happening. Our six-year-old, Brett, was still too young to understand, but we involved him as much as possible.

Before including her in the process, Alisha had been alone with her feelings and frustration. She kept them all bottled up inside. Afterwards, we often took Alisha and Brett to the library on our quest to find as much as we could about this type of leukemia. We tried to make it fun for everyone, and I know it meant a lot to the children.

## DOUG AND DEMETRA

My feeling is that when you first find out that your spouse is seriously or terminally ill, it is in the family's best interest to keep the children as well-informed and as involved as possible. Even though there were many questions we couldn't answer for our children, just talking things out gave them a release. It allowed them to feel free to ask us any questions they had about their mother's illness (even the little ones) and the possibility of her death and it prevented any walls from being built up between us.

I believe if you're not freely open with your children, it can backfire, since they're observant and will likely find out partial information from a friend or relative. Even though it may seem risky, you need to give your children credit for being able to handle the situation. If they don't believe you are being up-front with them, you'll lose all credibility as a parent, just when you, and they, need it most, even if you keep information from them with good intentions.

**Demetra's journal in June the following year:** *This evening I held Sean and Brittany and told them Mommy doesn't have a lot of time left. Sean thought the medicine would help, but I said they haven't come out with a medicine good enough to help Mommy. Later Sean asked Daddy if he (Doug) was going to die and what if he did, who'd take care of Sean? I really try to avoid starting to cry, but at times like this, I get a lump in my throat and a headache.*

**Two days later:** *Heather and I had another discussion tonight. I told her to look for small things to be thankful for and small things in life to enjoy more. It's so easy to overlook small and even big things in nature and in life. I love these children too much to drag them thru agony along the way to my end. I don't want them giving up on life just 'cause their mom died when they were just children.*

# Chapter 3

# TELLING OTHERS

**DOUG AND DEMETRA**

I called my family about Demetra's breast cancer. I remember it was awkward at first. I stumbled around, feeling at a loss for words. At first, I don't even think they really knew what I was trying to tell them. I do remember that in these initial conversations with my parents, brother, and sister, I was stoic. It was a fact that Demetra had cancer, that she was going to have surgery, and that she was going to undergo chemotherapy. I knew the reality of it all, but I was not good at communicating it. In retrospect, I know I showed no emotion in those phone calls. But let me tell you, I was terrified. I wondered how Demetra felt as she tried to explain her illness to her family and friends.

Although we realized it was serious, at that point no one in her family or mine thought that Demetra would die. In our minds, death could not and would not be a part of the illness. Yes, it was cancer, but we would beat it. I did not want to even imagine not winning that battle.

As I reflect back on those conversations with my family, I think the most common reaction was silence. There was a definite hesitation on the phone, and a sense of disbelief that this was happening to a person as young as Demetra—a person they all knew so well as she came into their lives through our marriage. Demetra said she got the same response from her parents when she called to let them know. The idea that someone so young and so close to you could have such a serious illness catches you off guard, and leaves you wordless.

## DAN AND PATTY

I think it's not uncommon to block traumatic events from our minds, and this was one of those events for me. I remember making phone calls. I remember where I was sitting when I made them and to whom I was talking. I remember there were a lot of tears shed on both ends of the phone line, but I can't begin to describe the level of emotional pain we were all going through. This happy family, supported by a fulfilling marriage, seemed to be crumbling right before everyone's eyes.

We knew we needed to tell family and friends, but it was difficult to know what to say. Surprisingly, I think everyone we talked to was in a state of shock and denial, just as we were.

# Chapter 4

# QUESTIONING - WHAT DO WE DO NOW?

**DOUG AND DEMETRA**

After you have talked to your children, your family, and your friends, and have made a course of action for treatment, you enter a time of soul-searching, then more confusion. At times, Demetra and I felt totally lost. We had a million questions, and we felt completely unsure about what was going to happen and how we were going to handle it.

During this phase, you too may experience a lot of emotional moments that you cannot anticipate. I remember vividly the last time Demetra was able to nurse Laurel, who was still not even a year old. She had to wean her 24 to 48 hours prior to her surgery. This strongly affected Demetra because, she admitted, it prematurely ended that phase of her life and showed her the reality and the seriousness of her illness.

Demetra and I went for many walks and talked a lot during that time. She often asked me how I would react to the physical and mental scars she would incur from her mastectomy. I let her know unequivocally that it would make no difference to me. I believe talking about it helped us to deal with the situation and its possibilities.

Prior to that, we still hadn't cried together. Demetra may have broken down and cried privately when I was at work, but we showed no emotional release in front of each other. At night, we would often lie in bed and still be awake at three or four in the morning, just lying there. I think we both looked at our situation as so unbelievable that we hadn't truly come to grips with it. We were just dealing as best we knew how with what we knew was going to occur.

## DAN AND PATTY

Going for walks helped us a lot. I remember strolling along with Patty with the kids running all around us. They were so young that they didn't really understand the full impact of their mother's disease. Did I? As we were walking, I remember saying to Patty, "From here on, our lives will never be the same." Everything was changing – work, home, normal life. We had so many life-altering decisions to make and so much uncertainty about what lay ahead of us.

When we would go for walks, we would talk about how much we take for granted. Many times in the past, when I wasn't feeling well, I had said that I commonly took my health for granted. Well, this was different. This was so very real. Sometimes, the thoughts were so frightening. What would I do if . . . ? What would the children do if . . . ? Will this new baby of ours remember her mother if . . . ?

**Patty:** *One of my most precious pictures is of Brett and me standing against the freezer in the garage, with Brett looking toward me. He is leaning his head against my pregnant body. Brett was always such a mama's boy.*

It breaks my heart to think about that moment. I still have and treasure that picture.

# Chapter 5

# SEEKING INFORMATION

## DOUG AND DEMETRA

After Demetra's diagnosis, we wanted to learn all we could about breast cancer. We went to bookstores, of course, and also received materials from our general surgeon, the American Cancer Society, and the National Cancer Institute. Demetra looked into the possibility of having reconstructive surgery after her mastectomy. She wanted to know all she could about her disease. She had a very positive attitude; she didn't shun it or ignore it.

>  **Demetra:** *I finished Gilda Radner's book,* It's Always Something. *It sounded similar to what I'm going through . . . Last week NBC had a show called "Destined to Live" about women with breast cancer. After all I've been through, I think I'm a better candidate for "Destined to Die." At times I think I should just give up, but then I think of the children and Doug. What choice do I have? In spite of all that is happening, each day I thank God for the children and Doug.*
>
> **August 3:** *The lecture was on, "What is breast cancer?" I found out that estrogen receptor positive cancers seem to have a better*

*cure rate. Older women seem to be estrogen plus (+) while younger women with cancer seem to be estrogen receptor minus (-). I didn't fit in any of the groupings as I wasn't fat, I had nursed the children, and no one in my family had had breast cancer, although all four of my grandparents had other cancers. I was the one who fell thru the safety net.*

## DAN AND PATTY

After we received the diagnosis, we decided to learn all we could about the disease. Like I said, we made sure to include Alisha and Brett when we went to the library. They actually helped all of us a lot. I really encourage involving your children as much as you can with all of your decisions. As we found out more and more, they really got into the research and even thought it was fun.

**Patty:** *We had the right attitude. Even though they could not understand all of the information, they were really interested in it. I was determined that this disease was not going to take me from them.*

# Chapter 6

# MAKING TOUGH DECISIONS

**DOUG AND DEMETRA**

From the day we found out the lump was cancer, Demetra and I faced numerous gut-wrenching decisions. As far as the choices we had for her treatment, we based our decisions on both the information our doctors gave us, and on what we learned from our research. We seemed to have very few options because of her particular situation. Using radiation to reduce the cancer was never an option; it wasn't even offered. The only course of action was for Demetra to have a mastectomy and follow it up with the standard dose of chemotherapy.

We felt there was no alternative to surgically removing Demetra's cancer. Therefore, we made the decision with very little emotion, almost as if she were having a hangnail removed. At that point, we still didn't fully realize all the ramifications it would have for Demetra's life, my life, or our children's lives.

# DAN AND PATTY

For us, in addition to the trauma of finding out about Patty's illness, we had another huge concern. Because Patty was pregnant, we had to make a decision right away. Could she carry the pregnancy to term and have the baby without chemotherapy treatment? Should she have the treatment during her pregnancy and risk harming the baby? Would it be best to abort the baby now and begin the treatments? Might an abortion lengthen Patty's life?

 **Patty:** *We wanted it all to work out and for a while, we thought it all had!*

In spite of all our questions, the decision whether to abort the baby was relatively easy because we both wanted to go through with the pregnancy. That baby was something special between us. We would take the risks.

We also made the hard decision not to use any type of treatment during the pregnancy. The doctors wanted to wait until after the baby was born before starting treatment. Then they planned to use an experimental drug called Interferon. At the time, it hadn't been approved by the U.S. Food and Drug Administration and there were a lot of possible side effects including deforming the baby or even aborting the pregnancy. Therefore, Patty wasn't on chemotherapy, radiation, or any other drugs while she was pregnant. She didn't take anything but vitamins. She did not advance to the accelerated stage of the leukemia while pregnant either, so the doctors said that our decision to go ahead with the pregnancy and no chemo hadn't affected her health at all.

It turned out that we made the right decision, even though we'd been risking so much. The pregnancy went great, and we had a healthy baby girl, Danielle Patricia, who is still healthy today. We called her "our miracle baby." Danielle's first name was taken from my name, and her middle name was taken from her mother's. We were all elated when Danielle Patricia was born. It was as though Patty wasn't even sick. Once again, we cried. This time they were tears of joy. Danielle was the most beautiful little girl. We had our baby. Now our family was complete.

After Danielle was born, Patty went on Interferon to maintain her white blood cell count. We knew a bone marrow transplant was inevitable if she wanted to have a chance to live longer. The drug kept a cap on her counts for a year-and-a-half. When her counts started creeping up, Patty needed to find a bone marrow donor. All of her family members were tested in hopes that one of them would match. The process was emotionally hard on Patty as well as the rest of us. Patty thought there would be no way we would find someone who would match her bone marrow. One of them did.

*Patty: Thank the good Lord for my sister, Rea. Before the transplant, our lives went on as normal as possible. The hospital was full, and I could not go in for the transplant until a bed opened. We waited for weeks until my blood counts were at the point where I absolutely had to get in. I was on a waiting list, and we knew that at any time we could get "the call" to say they have a bed ready for me. That meant either someone was able to go home or someone lost his or her life. We got home from work one day and the phone rang. The University of Minnesota hospital was calling to say there would be a bed ready for me in three days. Instant panic!*

*Now it was time for the transplant. We were scrambling. No matter how organized you are, when you finally get "the call," an unexplainable feeling of panic hits you. Fortunately, we had everything pre-arranged for the children and whatever else needed to be taken care of. This is when you really have to rely on family and friends.*

*Most of the time, my sisters took care of the children right in our home, but sometimes the children came to Minneapolis with our babysitter. We tried to have them visit me as often as they could.*

The hospital was in Minneapolis. When we drove out of Brookings, our hometown, Patty and I looked at each other. We were both scared. Patty started to cry. I asked her what she was thinking.

 *I'm scared I'll never see this place again.*

We were silent, but we both had a million questions in our heads. I can remember exactly where we were when Patty said that. We were driving on the overpass getting onto Interstate 29 just outside of Brookings. What a defining moment!

## Chapter 7

# STAYING IN THE HOSPITAL

**DOUG AND DEMETRA**

When we entered the hospital for Demetra's mastectomy, reality slapped both of us hard in the face. Suddenly, it was all too real. While Demetra was being prepared for surgery, we held each other's hands. I gave her a kiss before she was moved into the operating room, and we both wished each other well. While she was in surgery, I sat in the waiting room . . . waiting.

When the doctor came out hours later, he said he had completed the mastectomy and had confirmed the cancer. It appeared to have spread into her lymph nodes and he had removed as many nodes as he possibly could. For the very first time, I acknowledged to myself that Demetra was in serious trouble, and that our future would be seriously affected.

**DAN AND PATTY**

Arriving at the hospital in Minneapolis, Patty spent several days having a complete medical workup, followed by radiation and large doses of chemotherapy. The radiation specialists came in and measured her prior to the treatments. The amount of radiation that would enter her body had to be precisely determined. The radiologists had to position her in the exact same position each time she was given a treatment. They put a strap around Patty's waist and lower legs to make sure she wouldn't move. When the radiation was being administered, I left the room and the thick doors were closed behind me to prevent any radiation from escaping. I wanted so much to rush back in there and rescue her before it was too late. I felt so helpless.

During each of her treatments, I would go to a waiting room and watch her on a video monitor. While the treatment was in progress, she had on music of her choice. She chose "Lullaby," a tune from a teddy bear she used to wind up and put on her tummy when she was pregnant with Danielle. We both knew the radiation was destroying her immune system, her reproductive system. We knew there was no possibility of having more children. As sad as that was, we felt it was necessary to help Patty defeat this thief of life.

After several days of chemotherapy and radiation, Patty was ready for the transplant. Her immune system was depleted. It was scary to think what would happen if any little germ would have entered her system. It would have been devastating. The doctors and nurses brought bags of Rea's bone marrow and prepared for the transplant. Surprisingly, it was very anti-climactic. All of this preparation and it comes down to transferring the bone marrow into Patty like you would if you were just getting an IV.

On May 27th, 1988, Patty had her bone marrow transplant. The transplant went smoothly and Patty felt great afterwards. We even had pizza to celebrate her new beginning. We decided that day represented her rebirth, so Patty actually had two birthdays every year after that—one on her birthday and the other on her transplant day.

## STAYING IN THE HOSPITAL

Our elation would be short-lived. Three days after Patty's transplant, while we were still celebrating her success, there was a phone call waiting for me from Patty's sister, Susan. She had called to say that during the night their mother died of a stroke. I was shocked and distraught. I was very close to Bev, Patty's mother.

Just then, the sitter and the children came around the corner toward Patty's hospital room. I quickly told the sitter to take the children out because I was so overcome with emotion. I knew it was going to be difficult to tell Patty and it would be better to tell the children later.

One of Patty's nurses, Debbie, showed me to a room where I could be alone. I lost it. I couldn't control myself. It was like a dam had burst. Here we were, everything was going so well with Patty, and now I had to tell her about her mother. I wasn't sure I could do it, but I knew I had to be the one to tell her. Debbie went with me to Patty's room. She was in great spirits, and I hated to bring her such horrible news. Patty and her mother had been so close. They even shared the same birthday. Patty took one look at me and asked, "What's wrong?" When I told her what had happened, I could see everything just cave in.

For a number of weeks after that, everything went downhill. Patty was losing her hair and had her head shaved. She was emotional about everything. I felt so bad for her. The worst was that she would not be able to attend her own mother's funeral because of her weakened immune system. She was confined to isolation. Even a minor infection could kill her.

The morning of Bev's funeral, I raced back to Brookings (four hours away). I took pictures and had the funeral videotaped for Patty. Considering how close Patty was to her mother, I knew it broke her heart not to be there.

## DOUG AND DEMETRA

While Demetra was in the hospital, our relatives and friends took care of the children. We made sure the children had an opportunity to visit during any given stay. They saw their mother with the IVs in her, and they saw the shots the doctors gave her. That helped them—even the little ones—understand and relate to what their mother was going through.

After surgery, Demetra went through the aches and pains of recovery and the effects of the medication. Her doctor told us that her cancer was in the third stage. That shocked us. He also told us there appeared to be a spot on her liver. It didn't take a medical specialist to tell us we were in a worse situation than we had realized.

After the doctor left, Demetra and I, for the very first time, broke down in tears and cried together. We wept for ourselves and wept for our children. That evening, she and I walked very slowly around the hallways of the hospital. We talked and we cried during our walk. We were so anxious about our future. We didn't know what was going to happen or what we would do, but we knew that our future was changing. We knew that we would most likely not be together much longer. It was just a matter of *when*.

> **Demetra:** *Even with the hard times, life begins to be something to enjoy and appreciate. Before all this difficult stuff started happening, there were times when life wasn't so easy to appreciate—at times it was such dull drudgery. Being sick, one really learns to appreciate health, love, family, and nature.*

# Chapter 8

# UNDERGOING TREATMENT

**DOUG AND DEMETRA**

My most vivid memory of Demetra's chemotherapy treatments was her hair loss, probably because it was so obvious and noticeable. I think that really made the severity of her situation clear for the older children. Demetra had always had long hair that fell below her waist, in which she took great pride. Heather, our oldest daughter, had long hair as well, which she modeled after her mother's. Demetra told Heather that she was going to have her hair cut to about shoulder length before starting chemo. For the first time, Heather truly realized how sick her mom was. It was a major event in Demetra's life to cut off her beautiful long hair. Before the appointment, she had her hair braided and gave each child a lock to remind them of her flowing hair.

Shortly after her first chemo treatment, Demetra lost all of her hair. It never really got the chance to grow back before she died. It may have been an inch long at the most. She was on chemo from a week after her mastectomy until right before her death.

Demetra never got very nauseous from her chemo. Her medication for nausea and treatments helped her a great deal. She did experience other side effects though, such as numerous mouth sores and weight loss. She also suffered ear infections after the chemo started. She even had to have microsurgery on her ears because the infections would sometimes move into her sinuses and her teeth. When she had to have surgery, her white blood cell counts would drop, and she would become very, very ill.

We discovered another medical problem during Demetra's many treatments. At one point, her white blood cell count was so low that she had to have blood transfusions. Ironically, she almost died because the blood given to her was not treated correctly for IgA blood deficiency, a disorder we had not known that she had. Demetra's journal account of her treatments over her last months is like a warrior's diary.

**December 22:** *I have a Dr.'s appointment tomorrow to get my gums checked . . . She (the nurse) also called in a Nystatin gargle prescription. Evidently yeast in the mouth is a side effect of the chemotherapy . . . my ears are plugged and are bugging me. If it's not one thing it's another.*

**February 12:** *Tomorrow I get my bottom wisdom teeth out. The oral surgeon wants it done in the hospital as I have the mastoid infection, the IgA blood deficiency and the chemo to contend with. Getting rid of those two teeth should help with the chemo—when I hit the low counts (blood) my gums around those teeth swell up and are a source of infection . . . It's harder getting over the last bout of chemo and the infections. I'm on IV antibiotics at home. We do it at around 11 or 12 at night when Doug is home from work and he helps me then with this procedure.*

**June 3:** *In early May another CAT scan revealed my liver is in bad shape. The chemo I was on didn't work. As it is, the Dr. thinks the December liver biopsy missed the liver tumor completely. My chemo was changed to a trial type of method. The Dr. said the cancer I have may be resistant to chemotherapy and none will work on it. Possibly a catheter could be implanted on the artery leading to the liver for a direct transmission of chemotherapy. He said that would be a last alternative. As it is, the word "cure" doesn't exist anymore. All that can be done is to delay the inevitable.*

**June 18:** *I can't sleep. My feet and hands are swollen. My feet especially ache. I hope the Vinblastine isn't causing adverse side effects. I feel like I'm at least 6 months pregnant . . . The way I'm swollen it feels exactly like that.*

**June 19:** *My 33rd birthday. I had a tooth bothering me—I had it pulled because it would have needed a root canal and crown. I can get a false tooth later if I ever need it. I keep wondering if I'll ever see my 35th birthday; for some reason that sticks in my mind . . . I can hardly wait to be disconnected from the chemo pump tomorrow. It's hard sleeping at night with the pump as I usually sleep on my stomach. I also have to be careful with the needle. My catheter is so close to the surface, the nurses have to pad the needle with gauze—most people have theirs buried deeper but I don't have any place to bury it.*

**July 22:** *I have been in terrible pain since Monday. The Dr. ordered a chest X-ray. It could be a side effect of chemo. Guess I need a stronger pain medication—hope to get that Saturday.*

**July 27:** *I have doubts this new chemo is working. I'm discouraged as there are so many reminders of cancer. Last night on Lifetime, a show had a 30-year-old woman diagnosed with breast cancer. She* said she'd live, only losers die or something like that. It's depressing; I didn't ask for or want an untreatable cancer.

> **August 1:** *I'm dreading chemo on Thursday. I've really learned to hate that stuff. Those five days seem to last forever. When they stick the needle in my catheter it hurts more than I thought . . . the chemo pump makes such a clicking noise. At least Doug can sleep through it.*

> **August 14, about 2 A.M.:** *I can't sleep, so I will do some writing. The Vinblastine is bothering me some. Dr. Denes says it can cause paralysis of some nerves in the intestine, which probably caused my nasty aches in the stomach last time . . . on the good side my lymph nodes in my left side of the neck are going down.*

Much of the time we had in-home care, which meant a nurse would come to our house and give Demetra her chemo. When she was at home and suffering from one of her many infections, I would have to administer antibiotics to her at night through an IV device. The medication was distributed through a port-a-cath, which she had surgically implanted, like many people on chemotherapy.

## DAN AND PATTY

The first time Danielle came to visit Patty in the hospital—she was probably two-and-half. Patty was really worried that her daughter wouldn't recognize her or would be scared of the way she looked. It turned out to be a really good visit, though. When the children walked into the room, Danielle took one look at Patty and yelled, "Mommy!" Even though she hadn't seen her mommy for a few weeks, and had never seen her bald, she knew her mommy exactly.

Patty's immune system had been destroyed by the treatments and because of the strong treatments she had canker sores from the back of her tongue all the way around to the back of the other side. She had to brush her tongue with baking soda three times a day to try to prevent infection. It hurt me to see her in so much pain, but Patty always did what the doctors told her to do. She would do anything to improve her situation regardless of the pain.

## DOUG AND DEMETRA

Because of hair loss, Demetra wore a wig occasionally, but she found it uncomfortable and gradually realized that wearing one wasn't all that important. She wore it when we went out in public, mostly for the children's sake. But at home, she had a lot of fun with it. When the children came home from school, she would take the wig off and chase them around and play with them. She wanted to get them used to the idea that she had no hair by making a game out of it. I know the children enjoyed it. They made fun of her and she made fun of them. It was a way of easing the pain and dealing with the obvious physical changes they could see their mother going through.

# Chapter 9

# COMING HOME

### DOUG AND DEMETRA

Demetra was in and out of the hospital several times over the course of nine months. It seemed that every time she came home, we both were more exhausted than we had been the last time. In the back of my mind, and I am sure in Demetra's, we constantly wondered which hospital stay would be the one from which she wouldn't come home. Every time we returned from the hospital, we sat thinking about what she had just gone through and wondered what surgeries or treatments the next time would bring. It was not a question of whether she would be in the hospital again, but when, and what for. We felt like we were mired in quicksand. The cancer was slowly, but surely, pulling us down further and further, and there wasn't much of anything we could do about it.

### DAN AND PATTY

Patty spent two full months in the hospital and was finally released because her immune system had become stronger. Her homecoming required a lot of preparation. Since her immune system wasn't completely back to normal, we had to have the house virtually dust-free to eliminate as many germs as possible. Several of our friends came over and meticulously cleaned the house to get it ready for her. What would we have done without our family and friends?

Coming home was very emotional. My employer, 3M, had given me the opportunity to be with Patty at the hospital the whole time, so it was a homecoming for both of us. When we finally got home, the whole house, outside and inside, was all fixed up for a "Welcome Home, Mom" celebration. Family members and friends came to celebrate with us. It was great to see everyone, and it was great to be back together as a family again after so much time away.

# Chapter 10

# TALKING ABOUT THE FUTURE

## DOUG AND DEMETRA

Because Demetra and I communicated well, we talked about all aspects of her death, including our family's future, her not being around to be part of the future events in the children's lives, and even my possible remarriage. We talked about her funeral and her feelings about cremation versus burial. I said that I would agree to whatever she wanted. We discussed whether any extra attempts should be made to extend her life. We agreed that nothing could be done because she was terminally ill, and we didn't want to prolong her agony and the children's confusion. It was the day after we discovered that the cancer had spread to her liver that we started talking bluntly about our futures.

 *May 3: Liver scan results—I realize I'll never see Laurel turn five.*

 *May 3: (Letter to a friend) It doesn't appear I'll be one of the survivors of cancer. As a last alternative, a catheter could be*

*implanted on the artery leading to the liver for a direct transmission of chemotherapy. As it is, the "cure" doesn't exist anymore. All that will do is delay the inevitable.*

**May 16:** *It seems I may not have lots of time left. I'm having a hard time accepting the fact I'm dying. With my liver being cancerous, I don't think there's much to stop it.*

**May 24:** *This was Doug's last day of selling at Dillard's. It will be nice having him home . . . He wants to be home with me more since I won't ever get well—there is no cure in the future.*

**June 16:** *I really got Doug cornered with a tear one day—the first time I can remember. I said, "You know what I wish? I wish I could dream." Guess I should've kept that thought to myself. I no longer have any dreams, only wishes and thoughts of what might have been had I reached old age. There's nothing I would have loved more than being a loving grandmother and great-grandmother and also a crotchety old fart, which is a characteristic of some old people I have known. Old people are allowed the concession of saying what they feel and are excused because they are old. I'm really going to miss that.*

**June 24:** *This evening we did some shopping for our trip back to South Dakota. As we were going thru the Mall, it seemed like I was two people, one who felt well and another that is dying. The one who feels well thinks, yeah, children, I'll be there to make Thanksgiving dinner, and I'll be there for you always. But then the dying part of me, which is reality, gains control again.*

**July 27:** *I finally figured out how to explain how I feel. I know I'm still living, but the part of me that felt alive is becoming a ghostly image that I can see slipping away. For the first time in ages I'm really scared. It'll take some time to escape these thoughts. It's like my life is passing before me already.*

Demetra and I talked more than we ever had during these times and became closer than we had ever been. We learned a lot about each other, a lot about ourselves, and about what is really important in life. We agreed that it's not the things you learn in school, not the checkbook, not the savings account, and not the stocks and bonds. We realized it was relationships that are most important, not the possessions. We knew that the time was short and we wanted to make every moment count.

It was a very rich time in our marriage because we were as open as two people can be with each other. Our talks started the day they discovered the spot on her liver and continued up to an hour prior to her death. When she was lying in the hospital bed with an oxygen mask, we spoke to each other one last time without any reservations.

Our openness made the transitions after Demetra's death much smoother, even though it was still the most difficult time in my life. My recovery, my children's recovery, and my second marriage have all been much better than they would have been if Demetra and I had not had good communication during this very troubling time.

## DAN AND PATTY

Preserving memories for the future was very important to Patty. Before she went in for her bone marrow transplant, she made three videotapes: one for Alisha, one for Brett, and one for Danielle and me. In our tape, Patty talked about all sorts of things, including how tough it was for her to think about Danielle growing older and possibly being raised by someone else. Even though it was very hard to do, she also gave me permission to date and remarry because she knew it would be important someday. The children and I cherish those videotapes. They gave us a feeling that we had one last conversation with her. It is so important to have that final communication, whether it's a conversation, a letter, or videotape such as Patty made. For those left behind, it provides something they can always look back on and remember.

It's funny, but I can still see Patty running up and down the stairs in our house. She always tightly tucked her arms at her sides with her fists pointed up as if she was running in place. I will always remember the little things. Another thing I can't shake is how she used to say, "Hah!" All three of the children, to this day, do it exactly like she did. She always wrinkled her nose when she laughed. I'll never forget Patty and me dancing at the 3M 50's-themed dances that our company sponsored. The memories will always be there.

## DOUG AND DEMETRA

Before we were aware of Demetra's illness, she and I made a videotape together. That tape shows the children their mother as she was: the way she walked, the way she talked, and the way she styled her hair. It shows them the unique mannerisms and qualities of their mother that they can't get from still photos. I know they will continue to enjoy that tape as they get older.

## DAN AND PATTY

When nearing death, it's especially helpful if a mother talks about some things that may happen afterwards. Difficult transitions and changes in the children's lives such as Dad getting married again or their being raised by someone else can be easier if those issues are addressed before her death. They will understand that their mother wanted those things to happen someday and it's almost as if their mother is giving permission. The children will have a more positive outlook because they will not see it as their father betraying their mother since he and the children have her blessing.

## DOUG AND DEMETRA

Demetra made a point of talking to all of the children as often as she could, even during those last months when she was usually fatigued and spent a lot of time in bed. She took the initiative to talk to them about their futures, about sex, drugs, and alcohol and the very real chance that I would remarry at some future date. She told them that this was normal and that they should accept it. She also told them not to have an attitude of defeat or futility after her death, but to proceed with life and experience as much as possible, because nothing in life is ever guaranteed.

**August 1:** *I wonder what the second Mrs. DEO will be like. He'll have a harder time picking out #2 as he didn't have six children when we met.*

**August 14:** *I have several letters to write, hopefully I have tracked down one of my old girlfriends from high school . . . I also plan on writing a letter for Doug to give the second Mrs. O. someday. With six children, I figure he'll need a note vouching for his sanity. I love him so much, if I can do anything to help him, I'll do it.*

Demetra was able to track down her friend, who sent a letter back. It arrived the day after she died. Her friend, who also had had cancer, survived.

**Demetra, August 1:** *I told Doug today I wanted to be cremated, then he could be buried by his second wife—chances are I could be dead fifty years by the time he goes. A lot can be going on in fifty years. I hate the idea of being buried alone unless Doug and wife number two wanted a threesome. It'd sure make interesting reading for those who tour cemeteries.*

## TALKING ABOUT THE FUTURE

A few weeks before Demetra's death, she made a list of things she would like to do, or see her children do. However, she never was able to see, or do the following:

- *Teach Laurel to go up and down stairs.*
- *Potty train Laurel.*
- *Teach ABC's to Brittany.*
- *Teach Heather how to use a sewing machine.*
- *Teach Erik and Heather to use the Kitchen Aid mixer and how to do laundry or how to sort clothes, etc.*
- *See Jaimie ride his bike.*
- *Witness Heather have her first date.*
- *Erik bugging Heather about her first date.*
- *Helping the children with their homework.*
- *Erik's first date and Heather bugging him.*
- *Heather graduating from high school.*
- *Jaimie getting married.*
- *Each of the children with their first heartbreak with love.*
- *See Laurel and Brittany go to kindergarten.*
- *Heather go into seventh grade.*
- *Erik get through elementary school.*
- *Jaimie and Sean learn cursive writing.*
- *Brittany print her name.*
- *Brittany tie her own shoes.*
- *What Erik chooses to do for a job when he is grown.*
- *For Jaimie to find happiness.*
- *Sean quit sucking his fingers.*
- *Brittany quit sucking her thumb.*
- *Laurel ride a bike.*
- *See how athletic Sean becomes.*
- *See each of the girls in their wedding dresses.*

# Part 2

# DEALING WITH OUR WIVES' DEATHS

Ecclesiastes 3:4
"A time to weep and a time to laugh"

# Chapter 11

# THE FINAL DAYS

**DOUG AND DEMETRA**

I knew this day was going to come.

Monday, I got a telephone call at work from Demetra's doctor. He told me that all her blood chemistry measures were falling and she had only forty-eight to seventy-two hours left to live. He recommended that all the children come and visit her that day because she could slip into a coma at any time and would be unable to talk to them. During those last couple of days, Demetra wanted to go home to die, but it was not possible because her condition worsened very quickly.

On Wednesday, we received another call from Demetra's doctor. I left work immediately and went to the hospital to talk to Demetra. During that conversation, we decided that she would not be cremated. She had changed her mind and wanted to be buried in Brookings, where we had met, dated, and married while going to South Dakota State University. We also discussed whether it would be a good idea to have two plots, one for her and one for myself. She said she didn't want to make my future life uncomfortable by obligating me to be buried next to her. In the end, she left it up to me, but asked me to play it cautiously. We also decided that she would not wear a wig in her casket, because in her final days she had been completely bald and had not worn one.

In retrospect, I find it amazing that we could discuss all these issues so directly and clearly. I think we were in shock, but nonetheless we were able to talk about them. It was all so surprisingly matter-of-fact. From my perspective it went so easily it was as if we were watching someone else on TV.

After that talk, I went home and talked to my two oldest children, twelve-year-old Heather and ten-year-old Erik. I took them into my room and told them straightforwardly that their mother was going to die in the next couple of days. They had known she was very sick and was going to die soon, but it was still a shock to them. They had many questions, and I tried to answer them the best I knew how. We all cried as we realized the finality of it.

Later that day, the children went to see their mother for the last time. After that visit, we wrote down some of the special things that Demetra had said to the children so they could reflect on them later. The following are excerpts of letters written by Heather and Erik, the two oldest, about how they felt seeing their mother two days prior to her death.

**August 28, Heather:** *This evening I was reading some parts out of a book I got. It's called,* **You Shouldn't Have to Say Good-bye.** *It's about a thirteen-year-old girl whose mom has melanoma, a cancer, and it's too advanced to do anything about. I've read the book, but I still cry. It seems to get sadder every time I read it. Why does my mom have to die? It's so unfair . . . I don't want Mom to leave. It's like Mom's getting ready to go on a trip. But this trip is different. Mom doesn't come back from this trip. She never will.*

*Sometimes I wonder what being dead is like. But you should find that out when you're old. Not when you're young. I'm going to miss Mommy.*

**August 28, Erik:** *Today I found out that my mom is probably going to die. I cannot get through that I may be without a mother for the rest of my life. . . . Tonight I went to see her. She looked very tired. I imagine she is. . . . I miss my mom. She has been in the hospital for about a week now. My mom's tummy was really big when I saw her. My dad said it was the cancer and that it is getting worse. My mom was on oxygen when I saw her. I felt sad to think she is dying. I have been thinking about what will happen. I have been with her for a long time. It will be hard to say goodbye. I wish there was something I could do.*

The next day was very confusing for me, and I don't recall much of it. Demetra's father, sister, and brother-in-law arrived to help us. My parents, brother, and sister also came. Not all of the family members realized when they arrived that Demetra had just a few hours to live. That night, I asked Demetra if she wanted me to stay with her because I felt that this would probably be her last night alive. She told me that I should go home because I was going to need sleep in the upcoming days.

The next day, I went to the hospital early. When I arrived, Demetra was quite pale. She was on oxygen and it was obvious that she had slipped considerably during the night. Finding it very difficult for her to speak, she wrote something on a sheet of paper and handed it to me. I was caught completely off guard when I read:

 *August 30, Am I going to die today?*

All I could think of to say was, "The game is over." In hindsight, it seems like a ridiculous reply, but at the time, that was all my mind could come up with.

For the rest of that day, I sat in Demetra's room holding her hands, rubbing her fingers and talking to her constantly. Our conversation was mostly small talk. She couldn't say very much because her throat was dry, and she was short of breath. The doctors didn't come in because there was nothing they could do. At various times, her father, sister, and my brother sat with us and talked to Demetra. I didn't bring any of the children that day. I had asked them if they wanted to see their mother again, but they decided not to.

About 7 P.M., Demetra became disoriented for the first time during her whole nine-month ordeal. She tried to pull out her IV's and get up and walk. She seemed to have gotten a burst of energy. We had to hold her down so she wouldn't hurt herself. Her outburst ended as quickly as it had started, and she was calm again.

At this point, she was on morphine and responded very little at all, but I knew she could hear us. Finally, she spoke for the last time:

 *August 30, I love you.*

I told her, "I love you, too."

Those were our last words exchanged. Shortly after that, she had her last morphine shot and sank into a coma.

I had been hoping that when Demetra went into a coma, she would die quickly. I was thankful when she died about two hours later. At 10:40 P.M. on Wednesday, August 30, Demetra O'Neill died as I held her hand. I believe she died with little or no pain, and I believe she died knowing she had tried her best to beat the cancer. As she died, I felt myself trying to breathe for her because it was so difficult to watch her and not notice any breathing. Even so, I wanted to let her go peacefully.

After she died, everyone else left the room, and I spent a few moments alone with her. Then I called my parents to tell them. I asked them to tell the children and bring them to the hospital if they wanted to see her. The five oldest children came. I decided to do this for the children so they could see the transition from life to death and understand that their mother did not die at the funeral home, where they would see her next. I had asked a family counselor to be with us to help answer their questions. They did have many questions about the various aspects of death.

In a way, this time at Demetra's deathbed was our private funeral. The public funeral that was to come in a few days was for extended family and friends. We removed her rings and watch, and the girls took out her earrings. It was a somber time, but there was also some appropriate laughter. It was a rich time for us and a good way to bring closure to the process.

## DAN AND PATTY

The day after Christmas, four years after Patty's diagnosis, she woke up not feeling well. She said she had a sore throat and was getting a cold. I had become familiar enough with her illness to know what her needs were, and I could tell that she was rapidly getting worse. I took her to the Brookings hospital and told the doctor that we had to get her to Minneapolis as soon as possible. The emergency team said we couldn't go right away because of the ice storm, so we had to stay in Brookings that night.

Early the next morning, we flew by air ambulance to Minneapolis. When we arrived at the hospital, Patty's Uncle Jim and Aunt Arlene met us. I was so grateful to have so many caring friends and relatives throughout this difficult time.

The doctors in the intensive care unit suspected a fungal pneumonia. They said it was a diagnosis that would be difficult to survive. A couple of days passed, and she got progressively worse. I was very worried and wasn't getting much sleep. Patty was only partially aware of what was going on.

In just a few days, Patty's lungs had filled up with fluid and her kidneys were shutting down. Patty's whole body was falling apart. I've never felt so helpless. I was watching my wife, who was the epitome of strength and courage, fight against a Goliath. This time however Goliath would be the victor.

Eventually, her situation got so bad that she had needed help to breathe. It was 3 A.M. The staff asked me to leave the room so they could hook Patty up to the ventilator. I went upstairs to another floor to take a shower. I had to do something. Seeing Patty's condition then, and to this day, is one of my worst memories. When a person initially has a ventilator tube down their throat, their gag reflexes work to try to remove it. Patty was literally choking on the ventilator tube. They gave her some drugs to sedate her and make her more comfortable, but she still seemed to be getting worse. The results of the tests showed that Patty did indeed have fungal pneumonia. When the doctors told me, I felt that Patty had just received her death sentence.

Patty was conscious one last time a couple of days before she died. Our friends Susan and Debbie were with us. I was holding Patty's hand. She couldn't talk because of the ventilator, but she seemed very alert. Patty would squeeze my hand and smile at me. It seemed as though she was at peace and was ready to step into eternity. I can't remember how long Patty was awake, but it was probably no more than ten minutes. It was very memorable to see her smile and talk to us by squeezing my hand. It was as though we were having our last conversation.

From then on, Patty was so sedated that she was comatose. The doctors asked me if I wanted to put her on kidney dialysis even though they said it probably wouldn't do any good. I thought she had suffered enough. There didn't seem to be any sense in going on; for Patty, it didn't seem fair.

Our family met with the doctor, and he said it wouldn't be long before she would slip away. We all sat by her side, waiting for the inevitable. But Patty's heart was so strong, the minutes turned into hours. I remember looking at Dale, Patty's father. You could see the agony on his face as we sat there waiting for her to die. Finally, the doctor decreased her ventilator rate to deliver oxygen to her only when she needed it. About fifteen minutes later, Patty passed away. At 9:40 P.M., on January 9, Patty's battle with leukemia was over. She had gone Home.

When Patty died, Brett was sitting on my knee and Alisha was sitting on the other side of her mother. I was holding Patty's hand, and I felt her last heartbeat. I looked at the doctor, who checked for a pulse and then nodded. Everybody knew that was it.

We all left the room and stood in the hall, crying and consoling each other. Then I asked if they wanted to go back in and see their mom one more time. When I look back on that decision, I regret it. The body they saw was not the same person they had known. Patty's body had deteriorated to the point that she did not even look like herself.

The family became upset when they went back in to see her because it was not the Patty they had known and loved.

After Patty died, the doctors asked me if I would be willing to sign a release form so they could perform an autopsy. They said it would be very helpful for their research into the disease she had and the complications she had encountered, especially since it was unusual for someone this young to have this type of leukemia. I couldn't make myself sign the forms. It probably would have been helpful for the doctors, researchers, and other leukemia patients, but I just couldn't make myself do it. The rest of that evening is a blur. I only have scattered memories of conversations and events.

A couple of days later, some of Patty's co-workers told me that they sensed that Patty had died on that January day. Even though they didn't know at the time what was going on in that hospital in Minneapolis, they felt there was a gloom or a haze over the whole Brookings 3M plant. Everyone was depressed, and they sensed Patty's battle was over.

It was difficult for me to accept that Patty's health had declined so quickly. She was doing so well after the transplant nearly four years earlier that we all thought she had beaten it. Then, just a few days after Christmas, she was gone.

## Chapter 12

# THE DAYS AFTER DEATH

**DOUG**

The day after Demetra died, I felt detached from the real world. I woke up that morning with my oldest son Erik sleeping beside me. He had wanted to sleep with me the night before and I let him because it was the only time he had asked to do that. That morning, I could tell the entire family was physically and emotionally exhausted. We were on the phone constantly, receiving and making calls. I wonder what people going through a tragedy did before telephones.

Also that morning, I invited the children to come to the funeral home with me to make the arrangements. I felt it was important that any of them who wanted to go could do so. All of the boys wanted to go, but the girls did not. The children and I decided what outfit Demetra would wear for her funeral. Then the boys and I, along with my brother and father, drove to the funeral home. Everything seemed strange and unreal. I know I was functioning and making decisions, but I felt so removed from the scene.

Thank goodness, we were able to make the funeral decisions in a very businesslike manner. Choosing a casket was one of our tasks.

When we looked at one casket that was white with red roses on it, one of my sons said, "Dad, we can't get this one, because Mom was allergic to roses." I smiled, thinking that Demetra would have enjoyed his humorous remark. We picked out another casket.

I had to find people to be the pallbearers and help with other aspects of the funeral. Because it was scheduled for Labor Day, many people had already made plans to be out of town and having fun over a three-day weekend. When I asked friends to help me with the funeral, they changed their plans immediately. I appreciated that greatly because I knew it took them away from their families and holiday.

Other than planning the funeral and memorial service, I remember one other memorable event that first day. When we came back from the funeral home, two of my daughters went out with my sister-in-law just to get out of the house and do something. Shortly after they had left, I heard a knock at the door. When I went to answer it, I found a police officer standing there. My first thought was that my daughters had been in a car accident. But the police officer had actually come to let me know that they had just arrested a man who had stolen my credit card and was using it throughout Las Vegas and Los Angeles, and he wanted to know if I wanted to press charges. It seemed ironic that they would arrest the man on that day because I had lost that card almost two years earlier. Demetra and I used to joke about how I had lost the card because of a careless mistake. It's curious to me how odd things like that can trigger memories.

## DAN

After Patty died, we spent the night in Minneapolis. The next day, I drove back to Brookings with Alisha and Patty's best friend, Dee. Brett and Danielle rode back with other family members. Dee and I had a really good talk on the way home and did a lot of crying. About halfway home, Bette Midler's "The Wind Beneath My Wings" came on the radio. Dee told us she always thought of Patty when she heard it. Ever since, that song has meant a lot to me.

When we arrived back in Brookings, many family members, friends, our pastor, and some of Patty's co-workers came to visit. Many tears were shed. It was the first time we had come home without Patty. The reality seemed so strange and it caused me to feel very lonely. During the next couple of days, many caring people called, visited, and brought food.

Thankfully, a big burden had been lifted from my shoulders as Patty and I had taken care of almost every detail before her death. All I had to do was arrange for the pallbearers. Good thing, too. I don't remember much from the day we got back until the memorial service. It was all a blur.

## DOUG

We planned to have Demetra buried in Brookings, but first we had a memorial service in St. Louis on the Friday after she died. We had moved there about a year and a half before she died. I was very grateful to all the people from the Kansas City and St. Louis offices where I worked. They wrote letters, sent cards, and helped out during this whole process. I thought it was necessary to also have a memorial service there so that those who had helped her through this whole crisis could have closure.

I agreed to have an autopsy done on Demetra. I was initially told that, because of the autopsy, Demetra's body would not be ready for viewing at the St. Louis memorial service. However, the funeral home director later said that her body would be ready for viewing if I wanted to, but I decided against it. Instead, we arranged for the hospital pastor, Reverend Ken Potsman, to give a talk. He and Demetra had spoken three days before she died and had decided what he was going to say at the funeral. During the service, he mentioned several comments she had made to him and some thoughts she had observed about her experiences in the hospital. In addition to a floral arrangement, there was a basket full of ribbons and helium-filled balloons. Every member of our family was represented by a balloon. There were three blue balloons for the three boys, three pink balloons for the three girls, a white balloon for Demetra, and a red one for me. I decided after the service we should let the balloons go to symbolize Demetra's death and our releasing her spirit. We cut the balloons apart and released them together. Incredibly, the blue, pink, and red balloons went in one direction, and Demetra's white one went another direction. We all noticed the symbolism.

## DAN

Patty always loved roses, so I had a casket spray made of roses. The casket was maroon, which was one of Patty's favorite colors. It was absolutely beautiful. I'm sure she would have loved it. I still have a rose from the casket spray in a safekeeping box.

Before Patty's wake, we set aside some private time for the immediate family. Because of how Patty looked when she passed away, I decided I wasn't going to have an open casket. Only the immediate family would view her privately. In hindsight, I really regret requesting a closed casket. Patty looked so good and it probably would have given a sense of closure to friends. After the family had a chance to see her, the children and I said our good-byes, and they closed the casket. A few minutes later, my grandparents showed up. I asked that they open the casket again because I knew that my grandparents would want to see Patty. Then we said our good-byes again. Danielle was so young that she really didn't understand what was going on. I took her to the casket, and she touched her mommy and said, "Bye, Mommy." Patty was buried wearing one of my favorite dresses. A picture of her wearing that dress is also on her tombstone.

So many people came to the wake that it seemed like it was never going to end. They brought flowers and all kinds of plants. I talked to so many people that it just all became a blur in my mind. I can't remember anything about what happened that night after the wake.

One of my regrets was that I had started to keep a journal the first time Patty was in the hospital, but after she was discharged, I had thought she was going to be OK, so I stopped writing and never started again. I really regret that because there are times when I would love to reflect on what happened, but I just can't remember the details. Sometimes, it's difficult to remember if you don't write things down, especially when you're exhausted and in a state of shock. If you write things down, you will appreciate them later.

## DOUG

The day after Demetra's memorial service was a day of transition. That day, Saturday, I would take the children to South Dakota for the funeral which was set for Monday. My parents offered to stay and help me with the children, but I wanted to do it myself. At this point, I realized I was solely responsible for our six children. I decided I had to be able to handle whatever circumstances came my way.

I told my family that I felt it was time for them to go home so they could rest and get ready for the funeral. After they left, the children and I were left alone in a place where we had lived for only a year and a half. All I really remember about that Saturday was packing clothes, getting the children's things organized, and starting the drive to Brookings for the funeral.

Believe it or not, the children were well behaved throughout the entire drive. If their mother's last wish was that they were good during this whole ordeal, she got her request.

On the drive, we were graced with a significant thunderstorm that occupied a lot of our time. The children and I had a great time talking about the lightning and the thunderheads. During that time, we also talked about their mother, and they asked a lot of questions about our future. What was I going to do? What were they going to do? Who was going to take care of them now that their mother was gone? I know they expected me to have all the answers to their questions, but I didn't have the slightest idea. Since Demetra's death had come so quickly, I had not been prepared with all the answers they needed. I assured the children that I would care for them.

## Chapter 13

# THE FUNERAL

**DOUG**

The children and I were exhausted and spent Sunday night at a hotel in Brookings. The funeral would be early the next morning. My brother went with me to the funeral home to make sure everything was ready, while his wife stayed at the hotel to watch the children. When we arrived at the church, it looked beautiful, with many nice flower arrangements. (After the funeral, the flowers were distributed to nursing homes and churches throughout the community. It felt good to be able to do that.)

All of the children had created hand-drawn cards for their mother, and I made copies of all of them. These cards were then put in the casket and buried with Demetra. I also put in a card that I had given to her on our last Valentine's Day together.

At the funeral, all six children sat in the front row of the church with my parents, Demetra's parents, and me. Her mother had Alzheimer's disease, so I don't think she fully realized that her daughter had died. I remember distinctly that I had one pocket full of Cheerios for my youngest daughter, Laurel, who was now fourteen-months old. She was well behaved, but I wanted her to have something to eat to keep her from getting antsy.

The funeral ceremony was brief, and when it was over, I had not yet shed a tear. I maintained my composure very well, but I felt I was standing on the *Titanic,* waiting for it to sink.

## DAN

The day of Patty's funeral I got up early and went to the church long before the funeral was to start. I wanted to make sure that everything would go smoothly. When all of our family members arrived, we had a little private service beforehand. I don't remember a lot about it, so I really regret not videotaping it. I also regret not taking a photo of Patty in the casket so if the children or I ever wanted to see how good she looked at her death, we could.

The church was packed, and the funeral service was very inspirational. Patty had made a list of the things she wanted included in the service and the minister did exceptionally well. The service meant so much, not only because of how Pastor Anderson conducted it, but also because Patty herself had helped plan it.

I have never seen so many people at a funeral before. What a tribute to Patty! During the funeral, a babysitter stayed with Danielle in the playroom. I thought it would be best to eliminate the potential for some sort of innocent outburst from Danielle such as, "Get my mommy out of that box!" To this day, I have mixed feelings about the decision, but I think it was the right thing to do because she was only three and wouldn't have remembered the funeral anyway. It's hard to always know what exactly is the right thing to do.

After the funeral, the family walked out the side door of the church. We didn't want to walk back through the church because we wouldn't have felt comfortable. Everybody would have been staring at us, so we walked out the side and went straight to the car. The children and I just sat in the car and quietly watched everyone else walk out of the church. We were completely silent. We couldn't think of anything to say and all of us were too emotionally numb to know how to feel.

## DOUG

Because Brookings is a small town and the funeral was on Labor Day, very few cars were in the funeral procession and the trip to the cemetery went quickly. I was struck by the respect and honor that the police officers displayed for the funeral procession. At the cemetery, we again released balloons. It was very windy that day and this time they all went up together.

I strongly recommend that after the funeral and the graveside service, family members and friends should stay and watch the casket being lowered into the ground and the earth being pushed into the grave. Seeing that brings closure and symbolizes the reality that the deceased is no longer with us. I think people commonly leave the cemetery while the casket is still sitting above ground, and they miss that necessary feeling of closure.

After the burial, we went back to the church and had the typical sandwiches, cake, coffee, and Jell-O salad meal. Everybody said their good-byes, and I thanked the people who had helped me. Then the children and I went home, alone.

## DAN

After the service, we drove to the cemetery. Patty was buried next to her mother. It was still difficult to believe that they were both gone. Most of the details of the burial itself are pretty foggy in my mind, but one event stood out. After the burial, one of my best friends, Jack, the kind of guy who never showed any emotion, came up to me and gave me a huge hug, and we both began to sob. That surprised me because I had never seen that side of him before. But on that day we both just let loose, and I think it was good for both of us. I knew then that he and a lot of people were hurting. Up until that point, I had hardly shed a tear. But now the shock had worn off and reality set in.

## DOUG

During the funeral, I truly began the grieving process. A desperate feeling of loss came over me. I thought about how our family had lost someone who was incredibly significant in our lives. I experienced death more intimately in Demetra's passing than I ever will until I die.

All of the elements of the funeral, including the wake, the donated food, the flowers and cards, are very important. Everybody has to express their love and concern in their own special way. It wasn't the form of expression that was important, but the thoughts and feelings they conveyed.

I believe that most people look at these ceremonies as morbid and difficult, and they certainly are that, but we have to remember that everybody is going to go through this someday. The problem with death is that the impact it makes on the living is tremendous.

# DAN

I tried to think of Patty's death as a celebration. Her pain and suffering were over. Patty was going to a better place. She never complained. Patty had been a good mother and wife, and she had made the most of her days on this earth. It is sad that Danielle has only the words of others and videotapes to remind her of her mother. I really feel Danielle missed out somehow. This was Patty—a mother, wife, and friend who dedicated herself to others. I'm proud to say Patty touched many lives during her short time on this earth.

After Patty's burial, we went back to the church for a reception. I talked to more people there, and we shed more tears. That night, many people came to visit at the house. It was after that night that things really changed.

## Chapter 14

# RETURNING TO LIFE "ALONE"

### DOUG

After the funeral, the burial, and the reception, you reach a point when there is no more cake and coffee. Your friends have gone, your parents have gone, and you and your children are alone. It was then that I realized the most difficult times were just beginning for me. Now I had to go home and build a new life without Demetra.

It was a long trip home, but the children were real troopers. We were all very tired when we got home. It had been just one week from the time of Demetra's death until we got back to St. Louis after the funeral.

The following day, I woke up wondering, "What do I do now?" I had what felt like a million questions. Where do I get help? What do I do with the children? What do I do about my job? How do I manage finances? How do I figure out insurance policies, and how do I answer the children's questions? How am I going to cope?

### DAN

After everyone left, I had the most intense feelings of loneliness I had ever felt. Up to that point, so many people had been around, and I had been so caught up in everything that the reality of Patty's death and absence hadn't sunk in. Now, it was just the children and me.

That night, we all went into my bedroom and sat around on the floor by the television. The television wasn't even on. It was a dark, eerie night, the first time we were alone without my wife and the kids' mother. We could hear the wind howling outside. It was very disturbing. We all just looked at each other and started crying. We couldn't make ourselves stop. We sat on the floor and cried together. We were shedding tears for so many reasons.

We cried for their mommy and my wife, but it was more than that. We knew that this would be one of our last nights together. Very soon Alisha and Brett would be going away to live with their biological father. So Danielle and I weren't just feeling the loss of Patty, we were feeling the loss of Alisha and Brett, and they were feeling the loss of Danielle and me. It was a very depressing night. That night will live with me forever.

Three days after Patty was buried, Alisha and Brett were also gone. Losing three-fifths of my family almost overnight was nearly too difficult to bear.

Patty had a conversation with the kids' biological father prior to her bone marrow transplant, and he said he would do anything he could to help including the following three promises if Patty were to die: 1) Not making the kids move in with him until they are ready; 2) He will work out visitation with Dan & Dani; 3) He will alternate holidays with Dan & my family. Unfortunately, none of those promises were followed, and Danielle and I hardly saw Alisha and Brett over the next ten years.

That was one of the challenges with Alisha and Brett not being my biological children. I didn't have any rights.

Another important challenge after a loved one dies—remember that after the funeral or celebration of life, many friends and family are around. Then, shortly after, everyone goes home. It gets awfully quiet. My suggestion for friends and family is to not forget about the grieving widow or widower. They need you, now, more than ever.

# Chapter 15

# GRIEF

**DOUG**

In my opinion, grieving is like throwing a super ball in a racquetball court. It just keeps bouncing in all different directions. It is oftentimes irrational and unpredictable. You never know what you will experience next. It's random and that makes it confusing, frustrating, and sometimes frightening.

During the grieving process, it is important not to isolate yourself from others. I took advantage of a hospital grief support group, and that was good. However, most of the men and women in the group were quite a bit older than I was and we didn't have a lot in common other than the fact that our spouses had died. Because of our differences, I didn't have as much interaction with them as I would have liked. Actually, some of my best conversations took place when people I worked with asked questions about what I had gone through. I felt comfortable opening up and talking with them.

Another tool that aids in the grieving process, in my opinion, is writing. A year after Demetra's death, I spent ten days writing everything I could remember about the previous year. It was a good way for me to commemorate her death, my loss, and my survival.

## DAN

The loss of the two children really added to our grief. It was not only stressful for me, but also for all of the children. I felt an incredible loneliness in watching my family being torn apart and I could do nothing about it. I just didn't know how to deal with it.

Reading Patty's journal helped me cope with the losses and the grief associated with them. She had started writing it when she found out she was ill and kept it going through her transplant. I got a chance to reflect on what had happened. It also helped keep the memories fresh and helped me deal with some guilty feelings I sometimes had about our marriage. I knew our relationship had been good, but after Patty's death, I had some guilt about whether it could have been better. Reading what she had written reassured me that our marriage had been really good, and she knew I was giving it my all. It gave me a sense of comfort and self-satisfaction.

## DOUG

A journal of your experiences, observations, and memories can help your children later in life. As they mature, they can read what you have written and truly appreciate what you and their mother went through. Each of us deals with grief and loss in a unique and personal way. When it comes right down to it, you as an individual are the only one who can understand your own grief. For example, when I finally did let go and cry (it was a number of months after Demetra's death), I would cry almost every morning while I took my shower. That was the only place I felt relaxed enough to let all my emotions out. I was totally alone there, with no questions from the children, no household duties, and no financial worries. I could just deal with my feelings of loss for a while. This really worked for me. It is important to give yourself permission to cry. If you feel like crying, cry: it's normal, natural, and healthy.

## DAN

Through this nightmare, I have learned the importance of writing a journal. Many people start writing journals, but they quit early on because they feel that they have to put something down every day. This is a common misconception. My advice is to write only when you feel you have something significant you want to record. When you look back on your journal, you'll be amazed at how therapeutic it is for you and, ultimately, for your children.

# Part 3
# STARTING OVER

Ecclesiastes 3:4
"A time to mourn and a time to dance"

# Chapter 16

# CHILD CARE

**DOUG**

Because I had six young children to care for and no immediate family living nearby to help, I had to find child care immediately. I called the Social Services Hotline in St. Louis to inquire about finding a nanny or daycare. They gave me some names. I interviewed about six people before hiring one. Then she and I negotiated her salary. It was a very expensive process, but well worth it. Unfortunately, this type of service isn't available in all cities. Another alternative would be a professional day care center such as Kinder Care.

**DAN**

Daycare was already arranged for Danielle because both Patty and I had both been working before she died. For fathers who have relied on their wives to arrange this, I would emphasize that you make sure to interview people and get their references just as you would if you were hiring them for anything else. You will be using babysitters often. I would encourage you to have a third person join you when you take the sitter home or have someone else take that person home. Several years ago, my brother-in-law gave me this advice. This will protect you against false accusations of sexual assault or harassment by the babysitter.

## Chapter 17

# BACK TO WORK

### DOUG

Going back to work after being away during the illness and the funeral was very tense and stressful both for me and for my co-workers. Most of my co-workers didn't know how to react to my loss. They felt uncomfortable being around me. It seemed as though they were imagining themselves in my situation. Some tried to avoid me, while others expressed their feelings of regret and sympathy. Most really didn't know what to say. As a surviving spouse, I tried to be aware of other people's feelings and to give them time to figure out what to say and how to act, but most of the time they did the best they knew in an unfamiliar and awkward situation.

### DAN

It took time to get back into my regular work schedule. Even though I had some extra time off after the funeral, I felt numb and distant from everything and everyone. Fortunately, I had a very understanding boss. I found that the most important thing was to be honest with my boss and my co-workers. I think it's good to let them know that you're going through a tough time. Reassure them that you are working through the grieving process, but it will take some time. Let them know how much you appreciate their support and understanding. I also deeply appreciated what 3M did for my family and me, not only when Patty was ill, but also after her death. They provided both the needed insurance and the time off. I think many companies are that way. It's definitely worth discussing with the appropriate people in the company.

# Chapter 18

# SCHEDULES

### DOUG

After Demetra's death, I had to rearrange my whole schedule. I had to get back into the routine of work, and I also had to take complete control of the household, which I hadn't done before. I had to schedule time for cleaning, taking care of the children, shopping, doing laundry, ironing, etc. It was very challenging.

### DAN

I now was Mr. Mom. Instead of relying on Patty to pay the bills, cook, give baths, clean, run errands, etc., everything fell to me. Fortunately, Patty and I had organized our finances just in case something might happen to one of us. Patty had created a journal with all of our bills. She listed the fixed expenses on the upper level and the variable expenses on the lower level. It helped me stay organized. I would highly recommend the same for you. Don't wait for something like this to happen to get things in order.

It's amazing how many people have said, "How could you do it? I know I couldn't have." I am absolutely convinced that anyone who has to deal with this can handle it because you don't have a choice.

## DOUG

During this period, I felt that my life was largely out of control. I wanted to take charge of my life, but it felt like trying to pick up a piece of mercury. Every time I tried to get a hold on it, it would move in another direction or split into smaller pieces. As I gradually learned to cope with all the new stresses, I felt a little more in control. But just when I thought I had a handle on something, it would fall apart. I had many setbacks, so I had to be very patient with myself.

I found that it was important to have realistic expectations. I had to be flexible for my own wellbeing as well as that of the children. After all, their lives had been dramatically changed just like mine. I had to develop a schedule that suited the needs of my family, but I tried not to rush myself. I tried to take it one step at a time.

Even though it was often subtle, I experienced implicit pressure from my family, friends, and especially myself. I felt a lot of guilt—whether it was about something I felt I should have done to help prevent Demetra's death or something I felt I should now be doing for the children. I finally realized I didn't need to blame myself for *everything*. I convinced myself that it was okay to take it easy on myself and after that things would go somewhat smoothly.

# Chapter 19

# BILLS

### DOUG

I was the beneficiary of Demetra's life insurance policy. With the money I received from that policy, I paid off all my existing bills except for the mortgage on the house. Being debt-free reduced the stress in my life. I invested the remaining money from the insurance policy in an annuity, which was then disbursed to me over a five-year period. I used most of that money for daycare, but it also helped with unforeseen bills. In this situation, wise money management and sound financial planning are a necessity.

### DAN

When a spouse is diagnosed with a terminal illness, it is important to immediately begin to plan for the eventual changes that will occur. Your family's financial situation will most likely change drastically. It is wise to obtain the services of a trustworthy financial advisor. If you don't already have a financial professional helping you, carefully interview and check references of any advisors you are considering to ensure they are reputable. Ask friends or relatives whom they trust and have a relationship with.

Before your spouse dies, you should assume full responsibility for the family's day-to-day money management, including paying the bills. Otherwise, you'll be in for a major shock. In my case, Patty had always taken care of paying the bills, so it was a new responsibility for me.

# Chapter 20

# PAPERWORK

### DOUG

The funeral home director advised me of the paperwork I needed to fill out and keep on file, such as the death certificate. I would suggest gathering all the important documents you have, even before your spouse's death if possible, and putting them in a safe deposit box.

When your spouse passes away, thoroughly check into any possible benefits, such as life insurance policies, survivor benefits, and Social Security, whether your wife worked outside the home or not. You will most likely receive Social Security death benefits for your children up to age eighteen. Any benefits you receive will help you with unexpected bills, which you will definitely have.

### DAN

Patty and I both had written down our insurance and financial information so if anything happened to either or both of us, everything would be organized and well-documented. Initially, I felt that writing down all of this information seemed so unnecessary, but it proved to be extremely helpful. After Patty's death, I thought

I was totally clear as to what claims I should file and what payments I should get, but I still found some of the paperwork confusing. For example, I didn't know what all the Social Security benefits were. I knew that the children were entitled to Social Security survivor benefits, but I didn't know that I was as well. As a result, I missed out on about $13,000 in funds I could have collected.

Credit cards are another concern. After your spouse dies, you will need to contact the credit card companies about any cards you hold in both your names. Let them know that your wife is deceased and ask them to remove her name from all the accounts so that you are solely responsible for them. You must also go through this process for any other joint documents, such as house and car titles or investment accounts. You will probably have to show proof of death using your wife's death certificate.

To cut down on your stress after your spouse dies, prepare as many documents as possible beforehand. Prior to Patty's bone marrow transplant, she and I both had our wills drawn up, powers of attorney created, and burial plots purchased. We also set up a trust for the children, which I then had no control over. The trust department controls how the money is invested and distributed, which I didn't really anticipate. You need to think those decisions through thoroughly beforehand as you may end up suffering some unintended consequences later.

## DOUG

Demetra and I had drawn up wills prior to learning she had cancer. We wanted to make sure that no matter what happened to us, such as an accident, our children and our property would be taken care of in the way we wished. If you haven't had a will drawn up, I highly recommend that you do so immediately.

I also recommend that you plan your funerals in advance. About a year after Demetra's death, I took out a policy for my own funeral. The casket has been chosen, the readings have been selected, and the funeral arrangements have been made from start to finish. However, I have made it clear that those family members who survive me will have input into my funeral. They know, for instance, that they have some flexibility if they want to change songs.

Also, I recommend you and your spouse talk about where you want to be buried. Some people decide to buy two plots, one for themselves and one for their spouse. There is no right or wrong way to approach this. Whatever decision you make as a survivor is absolutely right at that time. You can always change things later, but the decision you make at that time is the most important.

# Chapter 21

# PERSONAL BELONGINGS

**DOUG**

It turned out Demetra's will was somewhat vague about how she wanted her belongings distributed to the children. It specified that the wedding rings should go to the girls and other personal effects to the boys. Based on my opinion, I wrote down which specific items were to go to which individual and put the list and the will in a safe deposit box. In the future, when I want to disburse those items, I will remember who gets what.

I also recommend that you distribute your wife's personal belongings, rather than letting in-laws, friends, or other family members do it for you. You should not dispose of her belongings until you are emotionally ready to do so. Everyone reaches this point at a different time. I was ready to give them to Goodwill or to people I knew could use them just a few weeks after the funeral. It might take you a lot longer.

While I was going through Demetra's belongings, I found pictures and notes she had written when she was sick and that were meaningful to me. It helped me move through the grieving process and remember the good times and the bad.

## DAN

Before she had her transplant, Patty had made a list of who was to get her personal items. As it so happened, that proved to be very helpful. I felt it was my responsibility to make sure Patty's family and friends were given what she wanted them to have. Some of Patty's friends felt awkward about inheriting her things and others felt comfortable about it. It was difficult for me to imagine other women wearing her clothes. But it felt good to know that many of Patty's things would stay in the family.

## Chapter 22

# WHAT IS A WIDOWER?

**DOUG**

When Demetra died, some of my relatives and best friends related to me differently. No one did it intentionally, but they didn't know how to relate to a person who had just lost a spouse. Couples we used to spend time with politely shunned me. They were available for a short time after Demetra's death, but then they started to exclude me from their activities because they had been used to spending time with us as a couple.

I believe that subconsciously none of them wanted what had happened to me to happen to them. I became a reminder of a possibility they didn't want to think about. I understood and appreciated their perception even though it was very difficult.

**DAN**

One of the most difficult issues I dealt with after Patty's death was the social changes a person experiences when you are no longer "a couple." I don't know if family and friends realize how it affects you to be excluded. They may stop inviting you because they don't want you to feel uncomfortable, like a fifth wheel, but instead you end up feeling left out. I sometimes wondered if it was just Patty they enjoyed spending time with and not me. I tried not to become angry or blame them because they're not experts at this either. Who is, really?

## DOUG

I found it difficult to come to terms with being single again. I had been married for more than fourteen years, and I was used to always thinking in terms of "we." I would catch myself saying, "We are going to do this." Usually, the people I was talking to would catch this right away and sometimes I would feel embarrassed and uncomfortable.

The major problem for me was losing the role of a husband. I enjoyed being married, I enjoyed having constant companionship, and I enjoyed doing things with my wife in that "we" status. For me that was a very difficult loss. I exchanged the familiar and pleasant role of husband for the very unfamiliar and difficult role of "widower." It is uncharted territory because you have little or no guidance to figure out this role. You have no footsteps to follow.

## DAN

Before I became a widower, I didn't know anyone who was one. When most people think of a widower, they picture an elderly gentleman whose children have grown up. But young and middle-aged men with children at home also lose their wives. You just don't come into contact with them very often and many times when you do, you are unaware of their situation. It's similar to when you buy a car—you notice that type of car on the road more often. Well, when you become a widower, you become acutely more aware of other widowers around you.

## DOUG

It took me two years after Demetra died to fully realize the unusual status of being a widower. I had started to date again, and I went to a party with a woman friend. Nobody at the party knew who I was, so she was introducing me. As people usually do, after our introductions, we talked about our jobs and children. You could see their questions by their faces. If you say you have children and you're going out with somebody, people conclude you must not be married any longer. They assume you're divorced. As soon as you say that you are not divorced, they think you must be stepping out on your wife, and only, as a last thought, consider that your wife might be deceased.

## DAN

Virtually everyone who met me after Patty died assumed I was divorced. One evening I took my daughter to a basketball game. A man sitting near us told me how nice it was that I took the time to care for my daughter and take her to the game. When he asked whether my wife was working, I tried to not make him feel uncomfortable, so I gave vague answers at first. But he was persistent, so I finally told him my wife had passed away. Boom! The bomb dropped, and he clammed up. He hardly spoke to me the rest of the night. I could tell that he felt very uncomfortable.

Whenever something like that happened, I felt obligated to say, "It's okay." I felt that I had to reassure people that I could deal with it and I could talk about it. I felt that I needed to say things like, "It's not your fault. There's no way you could have known."

## DOUG

When I would tell people I was a widower, they would suddenly be at a total loss for words. At that point, I felt that I had to step in and "bring them back." I would tell them that my wife had died, and I was doing fine. Still, they were usually very uncomfortable. Most hadn't met anyone in my situation before, and they didn't know how to relate. I believe this awkwardness is caused by our society's avoidance of the topic of death. I feel that most people don't want to talk about death or acknowledge that it is a reality. I found that the topic of death created a feeling of distance between me and many of the people I met.

I believe widowers commonly put on a false façade for other people. When I found myself in this new situation, I felt lost and bewildered, but I didn't want others to know how confused I was because I had to have confidence in myself to keep going. So, right or wrong, I created a buffer zone to allow myself some breathing room while I adjusted to all the new roles into which I had been forced.

## DAN

I think that family and friends often had misperceptions about me. When I would meet them in a public place, like a grocery store, I would smile and talk pleasantly with them. When they asked how I was doing, I would usually say, "I am doing pretty well." So they thought I was dealing with things just fine. What they didn't realize was that I was miserable inside. Many times I would have loved to say, "I feel like hell! How do you think I feel?" But I didn't because I didn't want other people to feel uncomfortable. Instead, I kept trying to help them deal with *my* tragedy. I put myself in the position of trying to help others feel okay about my situation rather than allowing them to comfort me because I did not want to risk causing them to be uncomfortable. I often wondered if I was not being fair to all of them by hiding my feelings. It was hard to know. Now I can see it's always best to be honest.

## DOUG

When you become a widower, you are unsure of what's expected of you. It's even more troublesome for the people around you. They are just as lost as you are, and they're looking to you for cues on how to respond.

As I progressed in my recovery, I was frequently asked what it was like being a widower, what difficulties I'd had, and what had helped me. When I was asked these questions shortly after Demetra's death, it was very difficult to be honest and open. There were times when I just broke down because the loss was so difficult to talk about. It took time to become relaxed and comfortable describing my situation to other people. The more I addressed this issue, the easier it got.

## DAN

Generally, you probably won't be asked a whole lot of questions, since people feel so uncomfortable. If people do ask you questions, it's probably because you have encouraged them to do so. That shows people that you are comfortable talking about it.

# Chapter 23

# EMOTIONS AND STRESS

**DOUG**

I recommend that within three to nine months after your wife has passed away, you get a complete physical examination. I had been under tremendous stress, and I had not been eating or sleeping well. I was exhausted, and I knew I was more susceptible to health-related problems during this time.

And then there are the new conditions that can crop up. It seems that extreme emotional and physical stress may cause an unsettling experience known as "paranoid phenomena." If you have this phenomenon, you think you see the deceased person alive. I think this happens partly because you are exhausted, and partly because you seem to lose touch, ever so slightly, with reality.

I never actually "saw" Demetra, but I did have a very realistic dream a month or two after her death. In the dream, I was in the basement of a house. I walked up the stairs, which led directly into the kitchen. As I entered the kitchen, I saw Demetra standing at the sink with her back turned to me. Her hair had grown back and was long. She was looking out the window, washing dishes and talking to me in a very calm manner. I never saw her face, but we talked about things that made sense at the time. She told me things would be alright if I just remained persistent. For some reason that dream has stayed with me. I have never had another dream like it. It was very relaxing and reassuring.

## DAN

After Patty passed away, I had a constant fear that I too would die and leave Danielle with no one to provide for her. I didn't think the good Lord would do that to me, but the idea haunted me nonetheless. I don't get sick very often, but every time I had an ache or pain, I was concerned it might be serious. I also became so focused on the children's welfare that I became almost irrational in my concern for them.

That kind of attachment can make it hard for you to leave your child, even for a short time. The first time I had to go away for a weekend, it was really tough to let go and let someone else care for Danielle. It may not be possible to enjoy yourself the first time you are gone, but eventually you will need some time away from your children. Of course, it is difficult for you if your children start crying as you're leaving.

## DOUG

Allowing me to take some time away from my children was one of the first steps I took on the road to recovery. When the opportunity presented itself and I felt I was ready, I tried it and enjoyed it as much as I could.

## DAN

I noticed that I started practicing what I call "self-imposed loneliness," or intentionally distancing myself from others. For example, when I was invited to weddings, I didn't want to go because I didn't want to witness the couple's happiness. It was difficult to see the happiness in others that I once had and that now was gone. When I would see a couple holding hands or going out for dinner or doing something she and I used to do, it would really hurt, and I would immediately look away. When I watched TV and came across a program that showed intimacy or affection, I would immediately change the channel. I rented a movie titled *Tequila Sunrise,* but I couldn't bear to watch it because of the painful memories it brought to mind. This is perfectly natural and it takes time to get over that feeling.

Eventually, I moved beyond my desire for self-imposed loneliness. It was difficult, but I had to get beyond it. I told myself this was ridiculous. I couldn't cut myself off completely from other people. Life does go on; others are enjoying life and meeting people. I told myself that I could—and must—do likewise.

## DOUG

When Demetra died, it seemed that my life was now like a whole new book with nothing written in it. Every time I did something without her, I was writing a new paragraph or chapter from scratch. I needed to be flexible and open to lifestyle changes. At the same time, I didn't want to make changes before my children or I could handle them. Most counselors recommend waiting at least a year after a spouse's death before making any major life changes such as taking a new job or moving to a new city. I basically agree with this guideline, even though I did not follow it. About ten months after Demetra's death, I sold my house, quit my job, and went back to college to pursue my doctorate in sociology. Everybody has to make these decisions individually, but I think a year generally is a good guideline to follow.

## DAN

After Patty's death, I faced many temptations, such as drinking, spending money on non-essential purchases, and other things I wouldn't normally do. I was very emotionally vulnerable and was looking for something to make me feel better, so for a short time I spent a lot of money. I sought change. Danielle and I moved to Arizona and bought a home. In less than a year, we knew the move was unwise and we moved back to Brookings. I bought a new truck, a car, and new appliances for my home. I entertained frequently because I was using money as my way of dealing with the loss of most of my family.

My advice today is to keep thinking about your future. If I had followed that advice, I don't think I would have gone on my spending spree. It's ironic that several years later, I would be a partner in a financial planning company. Other temptations such as drugs, alcohol, etc. must be controlled because of your responsibility to your children. You are their sole provider and their primary moral example. You must maintain your standards and values during those weak times for the sake of your children.

Another change that can make this transition tougher is the temporary loss of faith or religion, which a lot of surviving spouses may experience. When Patty was alive, we went to church every Sunday and sat in the same pew. After she died, I didn't feel like going to church anymore. I think it was mainly because it was something we did together as a family, and it brought back memories I didn't want to deal with. But eventually, I was able to go back to church again, which helped me feel better about myself, and I think it helped Danielle, too. It's a blessing that I found my current Patty in church.

## DOUG

In addition to all the pain and loss, a widower may also feel some relief. This is common, and you should not feel guilty about it. When Demetra died, I felt somewhat relieved for a lot of reasons, but mostly because I had known it was inevitable. Her illness had affected everybody we knew, and finally we could all move on with our lives. I could start the process of establishing a new life for my children and myself.

## DAN

There was a time in Patty's illness when we thought the worst was behind her and she was going to live a long healthy life. Then, one day she got sick and a few days later she was gone. If I felt any relief at all, it was just because she didn't have to suffer any more towards the end. I wasn't relieved for myself or for the family; it was too difficult for everyone. It was too big a loss.

## DOUG

To accept a diagnosis of terminal illness is just the first step of the process. When death actually occurs, even though you think you're prepared, it is still a shock, and I don't believe anyone is ever truly ready for it. Since I knew Demetra was terminal, we had the opportunity to prepare together for her death. In that sense, it wasn't like a death when everything suddenly and unexpectedly avalanches on you. Yet, even though we knew her death was near, I had many of those feelings when Demetra's death did occur.

# Chapter 24

# SINGLE PARENTHOOD

**DOUG**

When you are suddenly thrust into the dual roles of single parent and single man, you may have real difficulties maneuvering between the two roles. As a single person, you have the flexibility to go out and socialize with people and to start dating when you're ready. You need that time without the children. However, I found that I tried to overcompensate for the children's loss of their mother and would, therefore, be hesitant to leave them. I felt I always had to be careful not to unintentionally do or say anything that would negatively affect the children in the future.

For example, you might innocently say something like, "Nobody is as great as your mom," or "I'll never marry again." When you make those sorts of comments, your children may take them at face value and then be confused later when you decide to remarry. You may have the best intentions, but your feelings may change as you progress through your grief and those statements will come back to haunt you.

Discipline, which is always a difficult matter in any household with two parents, can become a real thorny issue. I found that I had to be just as firm as I had been when Demetra was alive—even when I did not want to be. I had to be more open-minded and more open-eared with my children's comments and questions, but just as firm as before because I was their only disciplinarian and role model. Your children may try to behave the way they think you want them to so they will appear more favorable in your eyes. Or, they may rebel. Or they may vent their anger and frustration on you. It is difficult to handle that rage and anger when you are going through the same feelings. At times like that you have to bite your tongue and concentrate on what discipline is appropriate for the child's actions. You should also clearly tell the child why he or she is being disciplined. In general, try not to make exceptions or excuses because of the death.

## DAN

I believe you should be sensitive, but maintain a consistent level of discipline. You have to be careful because the children are going to be very touchy for a long time after the death. Having lost their mom, they could react very negatively to discipline from you, so you have to have a lot of patience with them. They are going through a very difficult time and part of your responsibility is to help them get through it.

When you start dating, be careful when introducing your date to your children, because they could quickly become attached. If it doesn't work out between you and your friend, it will be very difficult on the children. They may feel like they're losing their mother all over again. It can become a roller coaster of emotions for all of you.

I dated a woman for quite a while before I decided it wasn't going to work out. Danielle was crushed. We had been going to this woman's parents' farm often, and Danielle became very attached to the farm animals. Eventually, I bought her a hamster to try and soften the blow. It worked.

One year Danielle wrote a letter to Santa that was published in the Brookings Register:

> Dear Santa,
>
> My name is Danielle Gilbertson. I am seven years old. My mom died four years ago. So I would like a mother for Christmas most of all. I also want a Paintin' Dazzle Barbie and a V-tech computer and a puppy.
>
> Love,
>
> Danielle Gilbertson
> Daughter of Dan Gilbertson of Brookings

## DOUG

As a single parent, you take on a lot of duties that are new to you. For instance, most men haven't done a great deal of clothes shopping with their children. The first time you do this, it might help to take along a friend or relative who can answer some of your questions such as: What is a suitable price? What is considered stylish? What sizes do the children wear? What kinds of outfits do they need for different occasions? It's not a hard task, but a lot of men have simply never done it. It's just another new experience.

## DAN

I loved to take Danielle shopping for new clothes. It made me happy to see how cute she was in all the different outfits. Danielle was such a little ham. You find that some of the most trivial things will give you the greatest amount of enjoyment.

## DOUG

Long after their mother's death, my children still had many questions. Before her death, Demetra spoke to the children in great detail about her illness and impending death. She especially talked to our oldest son and daughter about how their lives were going to change. She explained that when she was gone, I would need all the help they could give me. She also told them that I might start dating again sometime. By doing this, I think she gave the children permission to talk about her death and about all the changes in their lives. That was a very positive aspect of our tragic situation.

If a parent dies suddenly and unexpectedly, the children will not have this opportunity. In that case, I suggest you ask the children to talk about their mother, to draw pictures, or to write about their feelings. Never deny them an answer to their questions. If they want to ask you something about their mother at any time, do your best to respond to them because you are the only source they have to help them understand their new situation. If you don't help them with their questions, they will feel shut out. If they feel shut out or ignored, you will probably have more problems later in life.

## DAN

My two stepchildren were taken away shortly after Patty's funeral, so I never had a chance to talk with them much about their mother's death. This upset me because I didn't feel they had time to grieve and go through the healing process they needed. Danielle was too young to talk about it much, but she did find her own way of dealing with it. Many times I would overhear her playing in her room with her Barbie dolls. She would often be dramatizing someone's death. I suppose that was her way of working out all the different aspects of losing her mother, sister, and brother. It was both fascinating and yet sad to listen to her play with these dolls.

When their mother dies, children often think that it's their fault and they are being punished for something they did. Several years ago, our family was spending some time at Brett's home for Christmas. Later one evening, Danielle and I were the only two sitting downstairs and she asked, "Can I ask you a question? Do you think Mom died because of me?" I was shocked at her question. I responded, "Not only do I not think it was your fault that your mother died, I am convinced that because of the pregnancy test, that gave her more years with us because of early diagnosis." You could see the concern and relief on her face. I couldn't believe that she had been carrying that burden with her all of these years. It's very important to have those heart-to-heart talks with your children to make sure there aren't any internal feelings you're not aware of. You have to make sure they know it's not their fault that they did not cause their mother's death. They need to be reassured that death is a part of life in an imperfect world.

You may find that the children are very concerned that you will die and they will be left alone. You'll notice this the very first time you leave them at home with a relative or babysitter for a business trip or other overnight stay. They may become very upset that something will happen to you. Assure them that even if you do get sick or hurt, they will be okay. Don't leave them wondering what would happen to them if something happened to you.

## DOUG

It can be very interesting to see your children's friends react to the situation. When my children brought friends to our home, they were usually very curious about the appearance and upkeep of the house. I'm not sure what they were looking for, but they would go through all the rooms and look at the pictures or try to find out who was doing the cooking. Assure your children that it is okay for their friends to ask questions because they just want to know what it's like not to have a mother. Encourage your children to answer any questions they're comfortable with.

## DAN

Your children will probably be fascinated if they discover that a friend's mother also has died. The first time Danielle and I visited Doug's house after our wives had died, his daughter Laurel asked Danielle how her mom had died. Danielle replied, "Cancer," and then asked the same question to which she replied, "Cancer." It was interesting to see how matter-of-factly they related to each other. Sometimes I think children deal with the situation better than parents do because they don't feel as inhibited.

## DOUG

When children do have trouble understanding death, I think it is often because their parents don't communicate with them. The children copy the adults around them. Sometimes, other children will have more straightforward questions to ask your children about their mother. This childlike openness and honesty can be good for your children. It gives them the opportunity to express themselves on their own level and deal with the concerns that are important to them.

## DAN

After a parent dies, your children may have other fears you would never have considered. Not long after Patty's death, her sister, Rea, had a baby. Danielle, then three, and I went to the hospital to visit Rea and the baby. As we walked into the hospital room, Danielle became very disturbed and desperately tried to get away from the room. She was petrified because the last time she had been in a hospital room was during her mother's final illness. I had to pick Danielle up and carry her into the room, so she would understand that not everything that happens in a hospital has to do with death. When we were in the room, she was fine. If you are ever in a situation like that, you should try to be considerate of their sensitivities. It could be very traumatic for the child.

## DOUG

Difficult situations may also come up at school. Many elementary schools encourage children to make cards for their parents for Christmas, Easter, and various other holidays. I made a point of telling the teachers at the beginning of the year that the children's mother had died. When they knew our situation, the teachers were very sensitive to the children's needs. On Mother's Day my children still made Mother's Day cards, but they addressed them to me because I had become their mother too. In these cards, they mentioned that their mother had died and that I was now "Mr. Mom." They were able to address the various holiday sentiments from their own unique viewpoint. I recommend that you let your children's teachers know your situation ahead of time.

## DAN

One year, my daughter came home very upset because her classmates were making Mother's Day cards, but she didn't have a mother to make the card. It broke my heart. Danielle adapted the tradition of writing a Mother's Day card to me. I thought that was very special, but it might have gone more smoothly if the teachers had known her situation beforehand. As a result, I improved my efforts to communicate with the school.

Most school registration cards or biographical sheets only have categories for single, married or divorced. They don't have a space for widows or widowers. I found that it was necessary to go to the administration and the teachers to let them know I was a widowed parent, and would really appreciate their assistance and understanding, especially when it comes to holidays or special events. By going this extra step to improve communication, you can help your children avoid the most awkward and difficult situations.

# Part 4

# DATING AGAIN

Ecclesiastes 3:7
"A time to be silent and a time to speak"

# Chapter 25

# DATING - ANXIETY

**DOUG**

Fear of dating isn't unusual for widowed men. Women say it's true for them, too. Usually, the root cause of this is not the process of dating so much as the fear that you will become close to another woman and she too will die. After what you've gone through, the fear of losing someone again can be overwhelming.

It is also difficult to start dating again because you don't know whether the relationship is going to continue. Even when you have no desire for a long-term relationship, it's still hard to think of going out with someone, getting to know her, and then having to let her go. You are probably going to be gun-shy, so you have to be very careful.

**DAN**

The experience of your wife's death can make it difficult for you to let your guard down. Consciously or unconsciously you think, "We start dating, we get serious, we get married and then she too is going to die." You ask yourself, "Do I want to take that risk?" Of course, the odds of that happening again are very slim, but it's a possibility that is all too real to you. You fear losing another woman you love, not to mention putting the rest of the family through it again.

# Chapter 26

# DATING - READINESS

**DOUG**

Demetra and I had talked about me dating. She wanted me to start whenever I was ready. For some reason, she thought I would be ready to date six months after her death. I *wasn't* ready then, and I wasn't ready a year after her death. I think the longer you can wait, the better off you'll be.

For a long time after Demetra died, going out and dating never really entered my mind, for two reasons. First, I was still coming to terms with the reality of her death. Second, I was working full-time, and I had six young children to take care of. Dating was just not a priority in my mind. But even if I'd had only one child, I would still have been busy.

**DAN**

After Patty died, I went to a counselor who recommended that I wait two or three years to start dating seriously, to make sure I had properly grieved the loss of my wife. He also recommended waiting five years before getting married again. This advice proved to be very helpful to me, but at the time I was pretty bull-headed and I thought, "Not me. I'm Superman. I can handle it."

It was only a matter of a few months since Patty died that I started to date. I regretted that for a long time. I went "dating crazy" for a while, but the dating led nowhere. I got into a couple of relationships where we got serious enough to start talking marriage. Fortunately, we didn't go through with it because I definitely was not ready. Everyone goes through the grieving process at their own pace, but I think waiting a couple of years is an excellent idea. It seems that many people get married on the rebound after a spouse dies, similar to what can happen when there is a divorce.

In hindsight, I see that I was leaning on many of the women I dated because I didn't want to be alone. When I got into a relationship, it would usually be great for a while and then I would start thinking about Patty and the relationship would dissolve. I would end up hurting the woman I was dating, and many times, Danielle as well. After a few of those experiences, I started to wonder what was wrong with me. Why could I not hold on to a relationship? Eventually, I realized that the right person had not come along yet, and I was still not through the process of grieving. I just needed more time to adjust and figure out who I was and what I was all about.

# Chapter 27

# DATING - CHANGES IN THE DATING SCENE

## DOUG

When I did start to date again, it was usually only once or twice a month. It was difficult to adjust to dating again because it had been more than fourteen years since I had been in that situation. Times had changed since then and the dating culture had changed drastically from what I was used to.

## DAN

As a widower, you find that dating is vastly different. It seems that there are many more hassles to overcome. For instance, if you're like most men, your wife usually arranged for the babysitter. Now, you're the one who has to call several teenaged girls to find one that is available. It can be frustrating. One night I called several different girls to babysit, but none of them was available. I felt like I was the only single male in the world home alone.

If it has been several years since you've dated, you may be surprised at the cultural changes. I felt very old-fashioned because I was used to asking the woman out and paying for everything. I found that women are much more assertive and aggressive these days. The first time a lady asked me out, it caught me off guard. When the lady picks up the tab at a restaurant, it might really floor you.

One time, I put an ad in the newspaper classifieds to sell some things. A lady I had met at the swimming pool where Danielle swam saw the ad and evidently connected my number with my name. She called to set up an appointment to look at the merchandise. I didn't recognize her voice. When she arrived at my door, I recognized her and realized that she wasn't there to buy my lamps.

Another time, a lady called to invite me to a picnic, but I said I was too busy. A few minutes later, she was at my door. I told her that I didn't have time for a picnic because I was packing up to move. Eventually, she left.

Another time, I received flowers from someone I didn't know. The attached note included an invitation to lunch. While we were talking at lunch, she started to describe the inside of my house including the exact location of the furniture. She also told me how nice it was that I would sit and read to Danielle every night. She must have looked through the windows of my home. It became obvious to me that she was not the kind of lady with whom I wanted to be involved.

I have shared these experiences to show you that you need to be cautious. The last thing you need is to end up in a bad relationship on the rebound. Be careful and take it slowly.

## DOUG

Some women may ask you out because you are a novelty among single men. It seemed that some single women asked me to go out with them because I was a curiosity, something they had never experienced. They wanted to find out what a widower was like, I guess.

When I let a woman know I was a widower, she usually took a couple of steps back because she was surprised at first and uncomfortable. If she asked more questions, she wanted to understand and learn about me. If she didn't ask any more questions, I didn't pursue it any further because I suspected that there was no foundation there upon which to build a lasting relationship.

I found that most women were more knowledgeable about divorced men and their problems than about widowed men and their problems. Any woman who entered my life had to realize that my children couldn't be passed back to an ex-spouse and that I wasn't a part-time parent. Any woman who got involved with me had to accept and understand that I had a very serious full-time obligation to my family.

Because of that, when I started to meet women that I wanted to date, I quickly eliminated some of them by how they responded to my children. Not everybody can walk into a relationship with a widower and his children. When they agreed to date me, they knew upfront that they had to consider not just me, but also my children. It is a very demanding situation and the women who are willing to accept such a challenge are exceptional.

## DAN

In one sense, the women who came into my life had an advantage over women who date a divorced man because they weren't competing with an ex-wife. The memories of my former wife were there, but those memories would be there in a divorce situation too. In my situation, those women didn't have the constant tension of the children going off every other weekend to see their mother. I think that was helpful in some ways.

# Chapter 28

# DATING - WE'VE CHANGED!

**DOUG**

Dating was also complicated because I was older than most of my dates and I had six children. I aroused curiosity in some of the women I dated because they wondered if I was looking for a mother for my children.

As a widower, I had to realize that even though I was physically the same, everything else about me had changed. Emotionally, I was a completely new person. I was experiencing a situation I had never experienced before. Ironically, if my wife could have seen me then, she would recognize the body, but in many ways she would not recognize my changed emotions, thoughts, self-concept, and approach to life. You are just not the same man your dead wife married.

That's why I presented a totally different personality to women than Demetra saw. Even though we were very close, there is more to me now than she knew. This often caused problems for my friends, relatives, and co-workers because they viewed me as the man I was before. I think people who had never experienced the death of someone close to them had an especially difficult time recognizing how I had changed. They didn't understand the changes I had gone through. I looked the same outwardly, but inwardly was a new man.

## DAN

As a widower, I think one of the most difficult things about dating is that every aspect of it brings back memories of your wife and the emotions and feelings that accompany those memories. If it becomes too difficult for you—if your dates leave you feeling down or sad—it may be too soon for you to date.

Eventually, your friends will probably have someone in mind for you who would "be the perfect match," and they will try to set you up. They mean well, but the person they thought would be a good fit for you may not necessarily be the person the new you had in mind. They only want to help you fill the perceived loneliness they see in you. They may not understand when you try to explain how you've changed.

## DOUG

When I would introduce myself to a woman, I would suddenly remember that I was a man whose wife had died, who had medical bills to worry about, and who was raising children. I probably had a very different set of life experiences than the woman to whom I was speaking. I tried to ease her into my situation, so she would not be overwhelmed by my experiences.

Generally, people are just not used to hearing about traumatic experiences. They usually need some time to process the life-changing events of terminal illness, death, and funerals. If you want to date, you have to be comfortable answering questions even though it may become emotional at times. It may be very difficult to talk about your wife because the memories may still be very fresh and painful, but you will have to be able to talk to those people who are interested. If they can't ask you questions, they won't be able to relate to you.

## DAN

When you're dating someone, I think you have to ask yourself, "How would it affect this lady if I talked about my deceased wife?" If she is really understanding and interested in what you have to say, you may have the foundation for a deeper relationship. On the other hand, if she doesn't like to hear anything about your wife, you had better reevaluate the situation. In general, though, it's not a good idea to inundate your date with all the details of a past relationship. Also, your children will probably want to talk about their mom, and if that bothers the woman you are dating, the relationship will probably not grow.

## Chapter 29

# DATING - MOTIVATION: WHAT ARE YOU LOOKING FOR?

**DOUG**

When I started dating, I just wanted to get out of the house and start socializing again. I felt that I needed to get out and meet people and to do that I had to be comfortable with myself. I had to be able to acknowledge to myself that I was a widower who had a large family of young children, I had lost a wife to a terminal illness, and that part of my life was complete. When I accepted those things, I felt ready to go out and start socializing. I was not looking for a mother for my children, but I was ready to go out and date as I had when I was in college.

**DAN**

You have changed since the last time you were in the dating world because you may have been married for ten years or longer, and now it's hard to know what to look for. You are going to have to be very open-minded because the lady that you eventually find might be totally different from your wife.

## DOUG

You need to realize that nobody will ever be able to replace your wife who just died. Come to grips with the fact that she's gone. All the unique things about her have all died. It helped me to envision a book. Demetra was like a wonderful, but short, book that I'd finished reading. You have to put that book up on the shelf because it's complete. You can't go looking for someone who has the rest of the chapters because there is only one person who was that book.

You will never find another person like your wife, nor should you look for that person. Not only is it an impossible mission for you, but it is also an impossible mission for the lady that you expect to live up to your memories of your deceased wife. And you have changed from the person your first wife married. The traumatic events that have happened since then give you a totally different perspective on life. So, it is natural for you to search for a person who will look at you differently than your wife did.

Your wife may have loved your fun-loving attitude or your desire to have long conversations about vacations and retirement goals. The new you may be a lot more introspective. Your goals are different than they were. Your concerns may now center more on God and the meaning of life.

You might also find that a lady you are dating has some characteristics that make her similar to your wife. But just because two women like the same kind of movies doesn't mean that the second lady is a carbon copy of the first. Your relationship with that lady will never be the same as the one you had with your wife.

## DAN

You will never find another lady exactly like your first wife. You can't forget her either. You have to consider whether the lady you're dating understands that and keeps it in perspective. It is important that the lady you date understands you deeply.

## DOUG

You need to be very honest with any lady you date. Let her know that certain events or anniversaries will cause you to feel down. You can also tell her that if she has questions about your late wife, or if something is bothering her, she can always talk to you openly. If you have a good line of communication about your past, present, and future with the lady you're dating, you'll have a much more enjoyable time plus you will continue on your road to recovery.

When you start dating, enjoy the experience and don't rush into anything serious. Moving too quickly could just add to your grief. As a widower, you are used to having a wife in your life. You may feel a sense of urgency to revive the lifestyle you once enjoyed, which makes you vulnerable to those who take advantage of people with their defenses down.

## DAN

If you have a nice car or a nice house, some women are going to notice. When you are dating a lady, I think you have to ask yourself, "What is she really looking for?" Don't rush things. If you get into a situation where you sense a lady is looking at material things instead of at you as a person, you need to end the relationship. If you get into something too quickly, it could be disastrous, both emotionally and financially.

## DOUG

If you're going out with someone who is willing to move forward with you in the relationship at *your* pace, you should consider yourself very fortunate. When a lady is interested in you for who you are and is understanding of what you've been through, then she will stick by you and gradually become a part of your life. In this situation, patience is one of the most important virtues you can have because you have to give her the time she needs to come to terms with your life and the role she might play in it. She is contemplating a major change in her lifestyle, not just marriage, but a marriage into a pre-existing family with strong memories of a deceased wife and mother.

## Chapter 30

# DATING - CHILDREN'S CONCERNS

**DOUG**

When you begin to date, you also will want to consider your children's needs. This goes beyond finding them a sitter, reminding them to do their homework, and giving them a phone number so they can reach you. You need to help them understand what you're doing and explain to them that this is a normal part of life for you. In fact, you will probably have to explain this over and over again.

Even though you feel you're repeating yourself, it's a way of reinforcing to the children that you are in control of your life. As long as you are honest and trustworthy, they will feel secure in the decisions you make, and they will realize that you are not going to abandon them. They have already lost one parent, so they fear losing you, whether in a car accident or by a woman sweeping you off your feet; thus the need to reassure them before you go out.

If you want to date, you must make it clear to the children that you are the adult in the family and that you'll do as you think best. If you are not firm with the children, they may begin to dictate your behavior or show little or no respect for the woman you are dating, which can create tremendous problems and stress. It isn't fair to put a woman in a situation where the children are out of control. As the father, you must be in control.

When you are a single parent, your concern for your children affects every decision you make. After Demetra died, I took on a very protective role. I didn't want to do anything to create another loss for the children, so I decided that there would be no more changes in their lives. I wanted to shelter them from any more pain. However, I gradually realized that I had to move forward and one way to do that was to date. It is not wise to let your children dictate whether or not you can date.

## DAN

It can be a very exciting time when you start feeling comfortable with dating. You start to enjoy again the socialization and companionship of a lady. However, you should always make sure that you are not neglecting your children. If you focus on your date and ignore your children, you're going to get loads of resentment from them.

## DOUG

As you start dating someone regularly, your children will start to accept her as an important part of your life and theirs. If you suspect that a relationship is going nowhere, you need to end it properly and provide closure for the children. Your children have experienced a great loss with the death of their mother, and the loss of another significant woman can be very difficult for them.

When you think you are ready to settle down with a woman, you have to get your children involved in your relationship with her. Provide opportunities for them to get to know each other and become relaxed around one another. Then she and your children can start to create a framework for a relationship. All involved must be patient because the adjustment may be difficult and time consuming.

## DAN

A major concern is how well your female friend gets along with your children. If you are attentive to the children, and she isn't, the long-term stability of your relationship may be questionable. If you express your concern, you may be able to work it out. It doesn't take long to find out whether she enjoys being around your children. If you determine that she's only interested in spending time with you and doesn't care to be around your children, it is in your family's best interest to end the relationship.

If your female friend has children, the process is even more complex. The Brady Bunch notwithstanding, blending two families can be very difficult. For example, I once dated a lady who had two children who didn't get along well with my daughter. All three of them were young at the time, and they had many conflicts. Another problem was that this lady focused all her attention on me, instead of the children. That was probably the deciding factor in our decision not to get married. If you date a lady with children, take plenty of time to see how everyone gets along before you got into a serious relationship.

Be especially sensitive around holidays. Relationship dynamics can become more complicated during the holidays because you will probably share your time with the other side (your wife's or significant other's side) of the family. This can become very challenging in a blended family.

You need to be honest and transparent when you meet women. Don't try to hide the fact that you have children. Mention it right away and talk openly about it. Don't try to impress your date by being somebody you are not. Your date has to know who you are and what you're all about. It's also a mistake to try to impress your children with your date because they may get the feeling that they are less important to you than she is. Your date also has to be honest and transparent to both you and your children because they will see right through anyone who's a fake.

# Chapter 31

# DATING - OTHER PEOPLE'S OPINIONS

**DOUG**

Dating becomes even more complicated by the many expectations put on you. The sources of these expectations include yourself, your children, your parents, brothers, sisters, in-laws, friends, and co-workers. It seems that everybody has an idea of when, where, and how you should meet the next lady in your life. That was one of the more difficult factors that affected my dating decisions.

**DAN**

Your in-laws may not be very understanding when you start to date. They may not be particularly excited about whom you take out. They may feel that you are being disloyal to your wife—their daughter/sister—or that no one you date will ever be as good as she was. Their loyalty is understandable. You may be criticized for what you do and how you live your life, but you have to remember that it is your life, not theirs. Your wife has passed away and her family has to let go of her. They have to move on, just as you do. Just remember, everyone heals differently. I think it would have been better for everyone if I had waited longer before dating. Usually, sound relationships only develop when you have had adequate time to heal.

## DOUG

In-laws must realize that the widower has to go on with his life. It's unfair for them to try to manipulate or control the widower's life. Unless they have been in this situation, they have no way of understanding or appreciating the challenges that he has to deal with. Others should be supportive and understanding of the widower. They may not agree with everything he is doing, but they must understand that he is trying to put his life back together. He may make mistakes and he may even fall flat on his face, but that is better than doing nothing and feeling sorry for himself. One of the biggest steps that the widower can take is to realize that he is ready to start socializing again, even if he is not yet ready for a serious relationship.

# Chapter 32

# DATING - SEX AND INTIMACY

**DOUG**

All your actions will be under scrutiny now. You and your date have to have clearly communicated moral standards. You have to be considerate of yourself, your date, and your children. If you want your children to be respectful and understanding of your situation, you have to be a moral person. This shows your children that you are not changing your standards even though your life has changed. This establishes a firm foundation for your children to build on, if you decide to marry.

**DAN**

The way you handle the sexual aspect of your dating relationship is very important to you, your date, and to your children. If you respect your children, avoid sexual intimacy and inappropriate situations completely. It may take a lot of self-control but it is well worth waiting until you get married again before you enter into a sexual relationship.

As a single parent, you are the main role model for your children. If you expect them to have good moral standards, you must model that in your life.

## DOUG

No matter what your moral or religious beliefs, you have to consider your children's welfare from a very practical standpoint. Each time they see a lady come and go in your life, I believe they experience an emotional loss. If you are irresponsible or immature in your dating habits, your children may lose respect for you. You have to be upfront and honest with your children if you expect them to trust you and your decisions. You have to be responsible because your children will eventually reflect your actions.

# Chapter 33

# DATING: THE KIDS AND THE NEW PERSON IN THE FAMILY

**DOUG**

It also is important to encourage your children to become involved with your girlfriend. It is usually best to ease your children into a relationship with her and to explain how significant the relationship is becoming. If you kiss her goodnight at the door before she leaves, you may have to remind your children that that's part of a normal adult relationship. When your wife was alive, you kissed her goodnight, and you're doing the same thing with this new lady in your life. Your children will begin to understand that your actions show that you are very fond of her. As they see how much she means to you, they will realize that this isn't a casual relationship and that she might become their "mom" someday. A kind of pseudo-parent relationship may start to develop at this point.

**DAN**

When you start dating the same person frequently, you have to make a conscious effort to show an inordinate amount of attention to your children, so they don't feel they are being neglected. When you're sitting on the couch with your female friend, invite your children to join you—and likewise with her children when you visit her.

When you get into a serious relationship, give some thought to the discipline role your potential wife should assume. It can be a very uncomfortable situation for her and you. The two of you should talk about what the rules are and how you usually enforce them. She needs to lay down the rules and expect your children to follow them. Your children have to respect her, just as they respect you.

## DOUG

When a widower remarries, the new wife will assume equal responsibility for discipline and the other responsibilities of parenting. She becomes an equal partner with the widower because of a mutual desire to have a two-parent family. This is an important transition for the children because they now have two parents again. The father relinquishes total control and the new wife takes on new responsibilities as a non-biological parent.

Before I remarried, I reminded my children that their mother was dead and that no one could ever replace her. I also explained that my second wife was to be respected and honored as a parent. Children need to clearly understand that their parents have equal status and that they must respect you both. They may argue or rebel, but you can alleviate some of the problems if you make it clear to the children that your new wife has the same authority as you do.

I don't like the word "stepmother." She can never be their biological mother, but she can be a parent that takes care of them, disciplines them, teaches them rights and wrongs, and shows them love and affection.

# Chapter 34

# DATING - SO NOW WHAT?

**DOUG**

When you have dated someone at length, and she accepts you and your children, then your children can accept her as their friend and build on that relationship. You are a very blessed man if you find a lady who can adjust to all the things that have happened in your life.

**DAN**

Regardless of your dating situation, make sure your children know that no one will ever replace their mother. Their mother is no longer here, but she is a special person to all of you, and she always will be.

On the other hand, if you do remarry, you and the rest of your family have to consider the feelings of your new wife. She will have an incredible impact on you and your family. Stepping into an already developed family is no easy task and it takes a special person to be able to do it successfully.

# Chapter 35

# NO LONGER A WIDOWER

**DAN**

It is my custom to look for the good in the bad, but it took a long time to sort out what good came out of this tragedy. What I found was that Danielle and I grew closer than before her mother died. We have also become very close to Alisha, Brett, and their families. We've all done a lot of growing up because we were forced to.

Danielle is now 36 years old, living in Brookings, the town where she was born, and enjoying life. Alisha has three children, Jaelyn Patricia, Grace Leigh, and Blake Richard. They live in Iowa. Brett and his wife Jen, have two children, Addison Patricia and Tavin John. They live in Nebraska. We're so very proud of our children, their spouses and our grandchildren.

One of the most important things that happened to me was that I remarried. Patty (yes, another Patty) is a very special lady who has been a very important ingredient in our family. She has also been very understanding and supportive of the time I have spent finishing this journey of grief.

One step in this journey was changing my career. After some false starts, I decided to pursue a career in financial planning. To me it was the perfect way to help others, and not just with their financial planning. I have even met a few widowers with whom I have shared some special advice.

Was it easy starting over with my work, especially when I was a single dad? No, I have to admit I stumbled a bit. I would catch myself thinking of Patty and questioning if my schooling at age forty-five was worth the struggle. Today, I know it was.

## DOUG

Thirty-three years have passed since Demetra's death in 1989. At the time of her passing, the children ranged in age from 12 years down to 14 months. Heather is now 46 and married. Erik is 43 and married. Jaimie and his wife have a son and daughter, both in college. Sean is 40 and has a daughter who will start college this fall. Brittany, 37, is the mother of three daughters and two sons. Laurel is 34, married, and the mother of two boys and one girl. An interesting side note is that while pregnant with her daughter, Laurel was found to have breast cancer—at the same age as her mother. She underwent chemotherapy during the pregnancy (and during the covid pandemic) and delivered a beautiful, healthy daughter

You can't go through something like this and not come out on the other side a new man. It was during this sojourn that I met, dated, and married a wonderful lady by the name of Mary. How do you express to someone the impact she has made on your life? Not a day goes by that I do not thank God for answering my prayers to find someone who could acknowledge my past and still want to share her life with me as my best friend and spouse.

When I look back, it is to learn from the experience. Part of the new person I became looked forward to continuing my education and I saw that I could apply my own life experience to my studies. So in 1991 I returned to South Dakota State University as a Ph.D. degree candidate in sociology with my areas of study being Theory and Social Deviance. I wrote my dissertation on the topic, "American Widowers with School-Age Children: An Exploratory Study of Role Changes and Role Conflict." It felt good to use this awful experience in my life to help others. Today I am teaching, writing, and giving presentations on the widower experience, always ready to chat with a student or fellow widower.

Though my life experience was difficult, challenging, and filled with doubts at times, I see that the challenge that yet needs to be addressed in another book is about being a stepparent. This, I have discovered, is no easy task. Mary, I want to let all those who read this book know that I understand and appreciate what a difficult job you took on. People don't realize how little thanks stepparents get. So, Mary, to you and all others who take on this challenge in life, I thank you as a man, father, and husband. You will not be told this enough times in a day, let alone in your lifetime. With you by my side, it's been a great journey after all.

Our hope and prayer is that this book will help other widowers, their families, and friends with some of the questions, dilemmas, and critical decisions they will face. Most importantly, we want the many widowed fathers to know they are not alone. Losing a spouse is a very painful experience, but it provides a terrific opportunity to establish a new and different type of relationship with your children because of the experiences you have gone thru as a family. We wish you the best and God bless.

# Acknowledgments

## DAN

It's been 33 years since the most incredible epiphany of my life and my children's lives. This has been an unforgettable event that brought two men together to address a cause. Doug and I met in a classroom at South Dakota State University. We discovered we had both lost our wives. These types of coincidences don't just happen. If it weren't for Doug pushing me, this chapter in my life would still be undocumented. First and foremost, I want to thank Doug for having patience with me and encouraging me to help complete this book.

My wife Patty and I worked for 3M (Minnesota Mining and Manufacturing) at the time of her illness. 3M deserves a big thank you. There couldn't have been a more understanding, supportive, and giving company. When Patty and I needed the time off, they were there for us. 3M made it possible for me to be with Patty for the five months she was in the hospital. When the insurance company didn't pay for the air ambulance, 3M was there. Thanks to Jack Yonkovich, who was the plant manager at the time, for his understanding, support, and corporate influence. I also can't tell you how much we appreciated everything the Human Resources Department did for us. Gail, Nancy (Buffy), and Ryce, you were terrific. Phil Hogie, who was my supervisor at the time, was extremely understanding and patient. After Patty passed away, it took me a while to get focused on my job again. Words cannot express how much it meant to me that you were so patient with me. I'm sure there were others who helped out that we didn't even know about. Thanks to a great and supportive organization.

When Patty was in the hospital, Janet Bailey Meyer, one of Patty's high school classmates, established the Patty Gilbertson Leukemia Fund. This helped a great deal financially. Thank you, Janet.

Thanks to Debbie Brisch-Cramer, who was Patty's primary nurse at the University of Minnesota Oncology Unit, and also the rest of the staff. Debbie, you were always there for both of us.

I also want to thank the doctors and staff at the University of Minnesota Hospital for doing all they could to save my wife and giving her the extra years she had on this earth.

How can I begin to thank all the family and friends who sent cards, letters, and money to support us? You can't believe how much it helped both of us to see so many caring people. Thank you for your thoughts and prayers.

We have had the best and most important group of friends you can imagine. We always had a lot of fun, and when it was time to step up and support Patty, you were there in force. Thanks Jack and Lona Hanson, Mary Jo Oines, Bob and Denise Christiansen, Gary (deceased) and Cathy Lakeman, Dan and Judy Hanson, Rich and

Dee Herrig, Randi (deceased) Johnston, Rich and Deb Thoreson, and so many others. Thanks so much for coming to see us, taking care of the children, and of course, the benefit dance. You'll never know how important you were/are.

Gary and Lorie Leland, my uncle and aunt, thanks for not only coming to see both of us at the hospital, but also inviting me to your home for a little break. That's what family's all about.

Jim and Arlene Culhane, Patty's uncle and aunt, were my main support. If it wasn't for them, I don't think I could have kept my sanity. They were always there, whether it was the hospital, the airport, or a short visit to their house. They helped me keep a positive attitude while I was with Patty at the hospital. Jim and Arlene even brought me groceries in the hospital. I am forever indebted to them.

Both Patty's and my family were always there when we needed them. We never had to worry about the children. You guys are the greatest, and I'll never forget it. Thanks to the late Dale and Beverly Cavanaugh, both deceased, for being a father-in-law and mother-in-law only most can dream of. Also, thanks to Patty's family: David and Carol Cavanaugh, Susan and Curt Ribstein, Sheila Cavanaugh, and Rick and Rea McKeown.

If it wasn't for my mother Donna Diedrich and grandparents, Sigurd and Gertrude Overby, both deceased, I would not be who I am today. In addition, I want to thank the rest of my family: late father Harlan Gilbertson, Garry and Dawn Leuning, Mike Gilbertson, Greg Gilbertson, and my late stepfather Martin Diedrich.

To Rea, Patty's sister, what can I say? You were the reason for her renewed life. If it wasn't for you, there wouldn't have been a bone marrow transplant. Thanks so much for being there for us. How often can one say that you gave your sister the gift of life?

The most important acknowledgement I want to make is to my family: my current wife, Patty; my stepdaughter, Alisha; my stepson, Brett; and my daughter, "the miracle baby," Danielle. Patty, only a stepparent can really know how difficult it is to step into the shoes of a deceased parent and provide unconditional love and support for the family. You have been amazing. Alisha, Brett, and Danielle, as well as the rest of your families, I couldn't have asked for a more loving family. You all give me such joy. You complete my life. I love you all so much, and I am blessed to have you in my life.

Finally, if it hadn't been for the understanding and the grace of our good Lord, I don't think I would have healed. You can get us through any challenge, and I am truly blessed. It's comforting to know that we can lean on You during good times or bad.

# DOUG

As Dan mentioned, we met because of a life experience that neither of us could possibly have predicted. We became the statistics that one always wonders about. How do widowers cope and move on with their lives after the harsh reality that life does not care about fairness? It was because of this reality that we must acknowledge those people who played a vital role in our dealing with and recovering from one of life's most difficult lessons.

I would like to thank all the people whom I worked with during those trying days. Those fine people worked for the Department of Defense Aerospace (DMAAC) in the now defunct Kansas City, Missouri, office and the St. Louis office that is currently known as the National Geospatial-Intelligence Agency (NGA). Your prayers, cards, cheerful words, gifts, and understanding for my sporadic work performance were never unappreciated and are remembered to this day.

Among the great people in a long list, I must thank a few personally in this book. To Joyce and Rick Wycoff, babysitting the children and your prayers have never been forgotten. Rick, I never said thank you for mowing our lawn on the morning of Demetra's memorial service. To Betty and Jack Dunbar (both deceased), you were and still are the "step-grandparents" that were always on call in St. Louis before, during, and after my family's life crisis. Thank you Mark (deceased) and Vicki Oswald for the hospitality you gave to us prior to the funeral. To John and Jean Devero, Chris and Kevin Schwab, and their precious daughter Emily, thank you for being there when I needed your help. And to John Terryberry (deceased), Leon Tucker, Robert and Susan (deceased) Hart and LJ and Martha Patton, and to all the other friends I have not mentioned I wish to thank you for all the prayers and help during my family's trying time. It was a joy and honor to have all of you as a part of my life changes, past and present.

To the hospital staff at St. Johns in St. Louis, Missouri, you were outstanding. To Dr. Pennell, Demetra's surgeon, and Dr. Alex E. Denes, her oncologist, thank you for your honesty and frank talk about the reality of cancer and of death. Reverend Ken Postman, you gave Demetra hope and counsel during her many hospital stays and as death approached. You told me that I could and would survive and be happy again. You were right; I have survived and am an extremely happy man.

To my in-laws, Kandee and Duane (deceased) Strand, and to Demetra's parents, Marion and Martha Greenfield, who both are now deceased, thanks is not enough. To my parents, Don (deceased) and Delores O'Neill, I thank you for your understanding of some of the decisions I made, which I'm sure at the time made no sense to you. Tim, my brother, and Connie Stone, my sister, your shoulders were literally there to cry on; what more could one ask from a brother and sister?

To my children—Heather, Erik, Jaimie, Sean, Brittany, and Laurel—it wasn't easy then, and I'm sure at times its still causes confusion and wonder, but you have learned as well as I that this is real life and not a video game. You are great children. Always be thankful for what you had and have; never live in sorrow or pity.

To my wife, Mary, what a wonderful wife and friend you are. Prayers do come true. You have put up with me during my doctorate program and writing this book. Mary, you have given me a wonderful life again.

It may have been the "worst of times," yet life has a way of saying to you, "Acknowledge the past but do not live in it. But relish in the here and now."

www.ingramcontent.com/pod-product-compliance
Lightning Source LLC
LaVergne TN
LVHW091544070526
838199LV00002B/197